Maximillien de Lafayette

HOLLYWOOD'S MOST HORRIBLE PEOPLE, STARS, TIMES AND SCANDALS

From the Stars who Slept with Kennedy to Sex Pests & the Casting Couch.

Revised. 5th Edition

Coming Soon by the Same Author
**Hollywood Sluts and Sex Pests
Studio Bosses, Directors, Actresses and Actors who are
the Scum of the Earth**

*** *** ***

Copyright ©2011 by Maximillien de Lafayette. All rights reserved. No part of this book may be used or reproduced by any means, graphic, electronic, or mechanical, including any and/or all of the following: photocopying, recording, taping or by any information storage retrieval system without the written permission of the author except in the case of brief quotations embodied in critical articles and reviews.
Published in the United States of America.
Printed by Times Square Press.
Date of Publication: February 14, 2011.

Maximillien de Lafayette's books are available in 2 formats:
1-Amazon Kindle edition at www.amazon.com
2-In paperback at www.lulu.com
http://stores.lulu.com/maximilliendelafayette

Author's website:
www.maximilliendelafayettebibliography.com
Listen to his radio show on the Internet: "Maximillien de Lafayette Show" at www.blogtalkradio.com Click on "Archived" to see/hear all the episodes.

See a list of new books by Maximillien de Lafayette at the end of the book.

Hollywood's Most Horrible People, Stars, Times, and Scandals.
Revised.
From the stars who slept with Kennedy to Sex Pests & the Casting Couch.

5th Edition

Maximillien de Lafayette

TIMES SQUARE PRESS
New York Berlin
2011

Table of Contents

- Erich von Stroheim's orgies scenes...19
- Louise Brooks "The Nymphomaniac Vampire."...26
- Sex was a game and a necessity to Brooks, and conjugal fidelity meant nothing to her...28
- Sex at fourteen!...28
- Louise Brooks in New York: A call-girl with unorthodox habits and lots of sex...30
- From one man to another...constantly!...32
- Louise Brooks in Hollywood: More sexual partners and lesbianism orgies...36
- Facts about this most unusual woman...44
- Louise Brooks' lovers and sexual partners...50
- 1924 Most Notorious Woman in America...54
- Fantasy in the 1920s...vice squad...gorgeous girls...fabulous legs and delighted audience...54
- Earl Carroll's "Vanities" show: Problem with the D.A., and New York Vice Squad!...55
- Faith Bacon...62
- Sex, old men and gold diggers...65
- The Earl Carroll check list...69
- Other Earl Carroll girls...70
- Hollywood's Stars and Celebrities Who Slept with John F. Kennedy's...73
- List of names of Hollywood's stars and celebrities who had sexual intercourse with Kennedy...75
- Exner: "I was crucified because I had had the audacity to have an affair with Jack Kennedy."...91
- Kennedy, his sex addiction, and national security.
- The President who slept with whores, Mafia's women, and Russian spies!...92
- Gallery of stars and celebrities who slept with John F. Kennedy, to name a few...94
- Mary Astor's Diary: Sex and lust...lovers and multiple orgasms...106

- Juicy erotic excerpts from Astor's diary describing her extramarital affairs and love-making. In her own words and writing...107
- Her most famous sexual partners were (To name a few)...108
- Headlines in the newspapers...114
- Mary Astor's most famous dates and assumed lovers (To name a few)...119

The "Sewing Circle" Concept...121
- The "Sewing circles"...121
- Hollywood's gay/bisexual actresses, 1920's to 1950's...121
- Eva Le Gallienne...130
- Alla Nazimova's "Garden of Allah", the Mecca of lesbianism, bi-sexuality and orgies. The official center of the "Sewing Circle", where hundreds upon hundreds of lesbians and bisexuals would spend long weekends scre...g and pampering each other, usually at the tempo of a band of musicians made from "neutered boys" from Ethiopia, who served the demanding participants with all sorts of fetish and repulsive sexual acts...131
- Orgies with de Acosta, Greta Garbo, Irving Thalberg, Hope Williams, Tallulah Bankhead, Bessie Marbury, and Eleonora von Mendelssohn...134
- Mercedes and her relationship with Marlene Dietrich, and Greta Garbo...139
- Famous bisexual and lesbians & members of the Sewing Circle...141
- Joan Crawford...145
- Dorothy Sebastian...147
- Marilyn Monroe: "Oh yes, Crawford. We went to her house from a cocktail party, feeling no pain. We went to the bedroom and went down on each other."...151
- Crawford had a gigantic orgasm and shrieked like a maniac...151
- Clara Bow on Joan Crawford and the running around town...152
- Clara Bow, raped by her father...153

- Lizabeth Scott...156
- Some of the Hollywood divas found strength in clandestine feminine romantic and sexual friendship...157
- Greta Garbo lovers and sex partners (Men and women)...174
- What it was said about her affairs and lesbianism, and who said it...177
- Anna Sten...183
- Marlene Dietrich's lovers and sexual partners...185
- FBI Files on Marlene Dietrich...187
- Copy of a cover letter signed by Edgar Hoover from the FBI files on Marlene Dietrich...189
- Marlene Dietrich's gallery of some of her lovers and sexual partners...190
- The most famous lesbians were...195
- Pola Negri...207
- Lilyan Tashman...213
- Hedy Lamarr...218

From the landscape of stars' homosexuality in Hollywood...221

- Are they gay? Homosexuals? Bisexuals?...221
- How to find out?...221
- Look in the "Doom Book."...221
- Homosexuals, Gays, and Bisexuals Male Stars (The most recognizable)...222
- Charles Laughton...226
- Laurence Olivier...227
- William Desmond Taylor...228
- Rock Hudson's lovers (Men and women)...229
- Out of the closet entertainers...232
- Young Clarke Gable engaged in oral sex with fellow MGM player William Haines...233
- John Wayne's use of casting sessions to seduce young male contract players...233
- John Wayne's seduction technique...236
- Phony Hollywood and fake "Latin Lovers"...240
- What a vicious circle of perverts, sluts and cheaters...243

- Harry Cohn: "Who do you think your wife is fucking tonight?"...244
- Hollywood is fake, and 80% of its major stars are equally phony!...246
- Tom Mix: A Hollywood's phony hero, a horse thief, and a deserter...247
- Rudolph Valentino...249
- Latin Lover, Ricardo Montalban, a real man!..251

Hollywood's nymphomaniacs and piece of meat ...253
- What it was said by Hollywood's insiders...253
- Hollywood's nymphomaniacs and insatiable stars...256
- Women: The most notorious ones were...256
- Clara Bow...256
- Some of Clara Bow's lover...258
- Grace Kelly; a nymphomaniac with an insatiable sex appetite...259
- Grace Kelly's multiple lovers, to name a few...268
- The Stud Sex-Maniacs... 269
- William Holden...269
- Spencer Tracy...269
- Gary Cooper...269
- John Barrymore...270

The Ziegfeld Girls who created a huge scandal!...27
- Prerequisites to qualify...274

A different kind of scandal...279
- The May Irwin Kiss: The First Kiss on Film!...279

The Casting Couch...283
- During Hollywood's heyday, the casting couch was a revered institution...283
- Olive Thomas' sexual skills and the casting couch...284

- Olive Thomas talking to Lewis J. Selznick: "So this is where I get laid?"...286
- Mack Sennett's Bathing Beauties casting couch?...288
- Who was the first casting couch director? Sennett, Zanuck or Charlie Chaplin?...288
- The Casting Couch!! Ouch!!...297
- Charlie Chaplin was probably one of the first stars to make systematic use of the casting couch for sexual gratification...298
- Chaplin's casting couch's stars and starlets, and sex partners (To name a few)...300
- Is the casting couch still up and running?...309
- Do starlets sleep with a lot of Hollywood studs?...309
- Do outrageously sexy things go on all the time at Hollywood parties?...309
- Hollywood Sex Pests...10
- Don Johnson...310
- Steven Seagal...310
- Arnold Schwarzenneger...310
- The Casting Couch big names...311
- The most notorious casting couch directors...311
- Howard Hughes Lovers and Sex Partners...320
- According to insiders, Hughes has slept with at least 200 movie stars. To name a few...320

Table of Illustration

- Kim Novak...4
- Harry Cohn...4
- Vivien Leigh...5
- Paulette Goddard...6
- An orgy scene from von Stroheim's film...19
- Gloria Swanson wearing monkey fur...21
- Director Erich von Stroheim, a genius and a pervert...22
- Erich von Stroheim...23
- Erich Von Stroheim (left) and Mae Busch (center) in a scene from the film "Foolish Wives," 1922...24
- Louise Brooks...26
- Flo Ziegfeld...33
- Louise Brooks...34
- Louise Brooks...35
- Notorious lesbian, Peggy Fears, Louise Brooks' sexual partner in steamy orgies with Charlie Chaplin...36
- Walter Wanger...37
- Lord Beaverbrook...37
- Louise Brooks with director/future husband Eddie Sutherland...38
- George Preston Marshall, in front of the Red Skins office...39
- Louise Brooks...40
- Notorious lesbian, Pepi Lederer...42
- Pepi Lederer...43
- Louise Brooks with the love of her life, Buster Collier, and Dorothy MacKaill, in a scene from the 1926 film "Just Another Blonde."...44
- Louise Brooks with John Wayne...45
- Louise Brooks...46
- Louise Brooks...48
- George W. Pabst...53
- Scene from Earl Carroll's "Vanities"...54

- Earl Carroll with his girls...56
- Peggy Hopkins Joyce...57
- The risqué and very controversial poster of Kathryn Ray...58
- Kathryn Ray...60
- Peggy Hopkins...60
- Alice Fay...61
- Protesting members from one of showman Earl Carroll's "Vanities" musical extravaganzas parade past Musician's Union Local 47's old headquarters...63
- Faith Bacon...64
- A beach censor arresting two women in Chicago in 1922 for violating the laws concerning proper beach attire...65
- Gilda Gray...66
- Dorothy Knapp...67
- The Earl Carroll check list...69
- Mara Corday...70
- Shirley Claire...71
- Earl Carroll Girls' Reunion in Los Angeles, mid 1980's...72
- Janet Leigh...79
- Mary Pinchot Meyer...80
- Mary Pinchot Meyer...81
- Alicia Purdom...83
- Ellen Rometsch, an East German spy...84
- Carroll Arms...85
- Durie Malcolm...86
- Durie Malcolm (1917-2008) at age 18...86
- Durie Malcolm circa 1960...86
- Judith Exner...87
- Jackie Kennedy and Lee Radziwill by John F. Kennedy Casket, 1968...88
- Inga Arvad...89
- Patricia Bowman...89
- Ellen Rometsch...89
- John Kennedy's lover, Judith Campbell Exner...90
- Sam Giancana (second from right), mob boss of Chicago, with the Mcguire sisters...91

- Mariella Novotny being taken into custody by the FBI...92
- Judith Campbell...93
- Spokeswoman for the first lady, Pamela Turnure...93
- Jayne Mansfield...94
- Audrey Hepburn...95
- Kim Novak...95
- Gene Tierney...96
- Marlene Dietrich...96
- Nazi spy Ingrid Arvad...97
- Angie Dickinson...97
- Angie Dickinson...98
- Mary Pinchot Meyer who was mysteriously murdered in 1964 and her diary of their affair ended up at the CIA...99
- Mrs. Hjordis Niven, David Niven's wife...100
- Peter Lawford...101
- Frank Sinatra...101
- Jayne Mansfield...102
- Mansfield and Tommy Noonan in the most repeated nude scene of the movie Promises! Promises!...102
- Jayne Mansfield with Sophia Loren...103
- Jayne Mansfield as a stripper!...104
- This picture is from the 1936 trial over the custody of Marilyn Astor Thorpe...106
- Rare photo of Mary Astor...109
- Greta Garbo and John Barrymore, in "Grand Hotel", 1932...110
- Humphrey Bogart and Mary Astor in "The Maltese Falcon," 1941 Warner Bros...111
- Mary Astor...112
- George S. Kaufman, the principal lover of Mary Astor...113
- Headlines in the newspapers...114
- Mary Astor with her child...115
- Mary Astor in court...116
- Mary Astor, Roland Richard Woolley and Ruth Chatterton...117

- A page from Mary Astor's diary, written in lavender ink...118
- Howard Hughes...119
- Gene Fowler...119
- Douglas Fairbanks...119
- John Houston...119
- Ben Lyon...120
- John Saunders...120
- Ronald Colman...120
- Dr. Franklyn Thorpe...120
- Sybil Thorndike...122
- Patsy Kelly with Basil Rathbone...123
- Lily Damita...124
- Winifred Rennie (left) and Patsy Kelly...125
- Director Dorothy Arzner...126
- Judith Anderson...127
- Claudette Colbert, a notorious bi-sexual, and member of the Sewing Circle...128
- Myrna Loy...129
- Eva Le Gallienne...130
- Alla Nazimova's "Garden of Allah", the Mecca of lesbianism, bi-sexuality and orgies...131
- Claudette Colbert and her lover Marlene Dietrich...133
- Mercedes de Acosta, the "Female Lover of the Stars"...133
- Bessie Marbury...135
- Ella Anderson de Wolfe...136
- Young Ella Anderson de Wolfe...137
- Eva Le Gallienne as Peter Pan...138
- Greta Garbo with Ukrainian writer Salka Steuermann Viertel...139
- Laurette Taylor...141
- Louise Brooks...141
- Peggy Fears...141
- Agnes Moorhead...142
- Janet Gaynor...143
- Gertrude Stein...144
- Joan Crawford...145
- Dorothy Sebastian...146

- Dorothy Sebastian...147
- Dorothy Sebastian with her lover, Joan Crawford...149
- Two notorious lesbians, Gwen Lee and Dorothy Sebastian...150
- Pre-code Joan Crawford...151
- John Crawford with her sexual partner, Barbara Stanwyck...152 Joan Crawford with her lover, Marilyn Dietrich...152
- Clara Bow...153
- Lizabeth Scott...156
- Katharine Hepburn...158
- Alla Nazimova, queen of lesbianism glam of Hollywood...159
- Alla Nazimova...160
- Oscar Wilde, one of the most famous homosexuals of the era...161
- Bisexual Marie Prevost with stocking...162
- Bisexual Claudette Colbert...163
- Bisexual Claudette Colbert...164
- Gloria Swanson...165
- Fifi D'Orsay...166
- Jean Acker...167
- Ina Claire...168
- Katharine Cornell...169
- Katharine Cornell in "The Age of Innocence" (1929)...170
- Alla Nazimova...171
- Nazimova with Rudolph Valentino in a scene from "Camille", 1921...172
- Phyllis Haver with Ben Turpin posing for Mack Sennett, for his famous series "Bathing Beauties"...173
- Greta Garbo...174
- Greta Garbo in Queen Christina, 1933...177
- From left to right: Greta Garbo, C. Aubry Smith, Director Rouben Mamoulian and cinematographer Bill Daniels (far right)...177
Greta Garbo with Aristoteles Onassis...179
- George Schlee with Greta Garbo...180

- Greta Garbo and George Brent in "The Painted Veil"...181
- Anna Sten...183
- Anna Sten...184
- Marlene Dietrich...185
- Marlene Dietrich...188
- Copy of a cover letter signed by Edgar Hoover from the FBI files on Marlene Dietrich...189
- Jean Gabin, the love of her life...190
- Claire Waldoff...191
- Anna May Wong...191
- Tallulah Bankhead...191
- Ona Munson...191
- Jean Arthur...191
- Lili Damita...191
- Edith Piaf...191
- Mercedes de Acosta...191
- Judy Garland...191
- Publicity still from The Masks of the Devil (1928), starring Alma Rubens and John Gilbert...196
- Dorothy Gish...197
- Barbara Lamarr...198
- Sylvia Sydney...199
- Mae Marshall...200
- Barbara Stanwyck...201
- Theda Bera: The screen's first sex symbol...202
- Gilda Ray...203
- Myrna Darby performed in the Ziegfeld Follies of 1927...204
- Marilyn Vega...205
- Pola Negri...206
- Pola Negri...207
- Pola Negri with Rudolph Valentino...207
- Negri at Valentino's tomb...208
- Emil Jannings, Pola Negri in the 1919 film "Madame Dubarry"...209
- Mary Brian...210
- Josephine Baker...211
- Hope Williams...212

- Lilyan Tashman...213
- Lilyan Tashman...214
- Lilyan Tashman...215
- Tallulah Bankead...216
- Kurt Weill, Lotte Lenya, von Rechts, Eleonora Mendelssohn, and Francesco von Mendelssohn in 1935 in New York City...216
- Lili Damita with Eric von Stroheim...217
- Hedy Lamarr...218
- Beatrice Lillie...219
- Sally Forrest...220
- Robert Taylor...223
- Judy Holliday, Jose Ferrer, Gloria Swanson, and George Cukor at an Oscar party in 1951...224
- Alan Ladd and Veronica Lake in "This Gun for Hire", 1942...225
- Charles Laughton...226
- Laurence Olivier...227
- William Desmond Taylor...228
- Rock Hudson's lovers...229
- James Dean...230
- James Dean and his lover Sal Mineo...231
- MGM player William Haines...234
- Clarke Gable...234
- John Wayne...235
- Randolph Scott with his lover Cary Grant...237
- Cary Grant and Randolph Scott; two lovers in a "cachette"...238
- Joel McCrea...239
- Montgomery Clift...239
- Ramon Novarro...240
- Gilbert Roland...241
- Antonio Moreno...242
- Bisexual actor Ramon Novarro and Norma Shearer in "The student Prince in old Heidelberg", 1927, directed by Ernst Lubitsch...243
- Ramon Novarro with his lover Gilbert Roland (left) 1930...244

- Harry Cohn with Judy Holliday during a dinner at the Cocoanut Drove...245
- Tom Mix...247
- Pola Negri and Rudolph Valentino last moment...248
- Rudolph Valentino and wife for a few months, Natacha Rambova...249
- Rudolph Valentino...250
- Rudolph Valentino romances Alice Terry in "The Four Horsemen of the Apocalypse."...251
- Ricardo Montalbán and Esther Williams in the film "On an Island With You" (1948)...252
- Kim Novak...253
- Harry Cohn...253
- Paulette Goddard...254
- Vivien Leigh...255
- Clara Bow...256
- Clara Bow, the "It Girl."...257
- Grace Kelly with Oleg Cassini in 1954...260
- Grace Kelly and Clark Gable in a scene from "Mogambo"...261
- Grace Kelly and Ray Milland...262
- The Princess...265
- Prince Rainier mourning his wife Grace...266
- Grace Kelly with Jimmy Stewart...267
- Grace Kelly is shown here in a black dress, in the front row at Josephine Baker's state funeral...268
- William Holden...269
- Spencer Tracy...269
- John Barrymore with wife Elaine Barrie...270
- Chorus girl Evelyn Nesbit...271
- John Barrymore with Mary Astor in "Beau Brummel," 1924...272
- Dorothy Flood...275
- Naomi Johnson...275
- Adrienne Ames...175
- Anonyma "Debbie"...275
- Marjorie King...276
- Jean Ackerman...276
- Muriel Finley...276

- The Cutter Sisters...276
- Vivian Porter...277
- Marilyn Vega...277
- Ann Lee Patterson...277
- Anita Berber...277
- And this what Hollywood's actresses (Beauties) do after hour!...278
- Thomas Alva Edison...279
- May Irvin being kissed by John C. Rice...280
- May Irvin...280
- Florenz Ziegfeld...284
- Olive Thomas...285
- Olive Thomas in the 10th episode of "Beatrice Fairfax"...286
- Sarah Bernhardt as Lady Macbeth, circa 1884...287
- Is this what Sennett was talking about?...288
- Mack Sennett...289
- Phyllis Haver and Gloria Swanson...291
- Chester Conklin with Mack Sennett's "Bathing Beauties."...292
- Mac Sennett's Bathing Beauties...293
- Marie Prevost...294
- Phyllis Haver...295
- Carole Lombard...296
- Charlie Chaplin's head...298
- Gloria Swanson, Charles Chaplin and Marion Davies at the premiere of "City Lights" in Los Angeles on 30 January 1931...301
- Hetty Kelly...302
- Edna Purviance...303
- Chaplin with wife Paulette Goddard...304
- Lita Grey...305
- Mildred Harris and Billie Dove in "The Heart of a Follies Girl" (1928)...305
- Fingerprinting Charlie Chaplin, like a criminal...306
- Joan Barry...306
- Joan Barry...306
- An attorney questioning Joan Barry...308
- Don Johnson...310

- Steven Seagal...310
- Arnold Schwarzenneger...310
- Ben Schulberg...312
- Charlie Chaplin...312
- Flo Ziegfeld...313
- George Preston Marshall...313
- George White...314
- Harry Cohn...314
- Howard Hughes...315
- Irving Thalberg...315
- John Barrymore...316
- Lewis J. Selznick...316
- Mac Sennett ...317
- Raymond Griffith...317
- Irving Thalberg, his wife Norma Shearer and Louis B Mayer...318
- Anita Page...319

An orgy scene from von Stroheim's film.

Erich von Stroheim's orgies scenes

Erich von Stroheim is the notorious and infamous director of "The Merry Widow", MGM, 1925.
Erich von Stroheim was asked to direct Mae Murray when he heard that the job was to go to her husband, Robert Z. Leonard. He appealed to the head of MGM; Louis B. Mayer became disturbed when Stroheim said that the girl would be a whore and he struck him, as reported by Kevin Brownlow.
Later on, Irving Thalberg fired von Stroheim and replaced with Rupert Julian.

Some insiders have claimed that three of von Stroheim's film, were full of obscene scenes of orgies and real kinky sexual acts. Author Anger wrote that that the orgy and bordello scenes Stroheim filmed were genuinely naughty...giving booze to extras and encouraging kinky acts.
Because of this outrageous obscenity, Louis B. Mayer and Thalberg fired von Stroheim.

Gloria Swanson would not admit that Stroheim did in fact shoot sex scenes using whores and homosexuals, but at one time, she made it very clear, that in "the dark corners of some scenes, somebody had screwed somebody..."

In fact, the alleged orgies scenes did not bother Swanson at all, for it was common knowledge, that Swanson herself was a nymphomaniac, a bisexual, and did participate in many orgies with female stars members of the notorious "Sewing Circle."
Others have said, that the faces of the extras (actors and prostitutes-actresses) were masked, and the reason for that, was to hide their identities, because they did no want to be seen on the screen "fucking each other."

Others have said that the players were not professional actors and actresses, but extras. Back then, the word extra meant many things including whores, and "Harem", Hollywood's harem, that is; another word meaning prostitutes. Everybody in Hollywood knew that the studios called these prostitutes "extras", because they did not want the vice squad to raid on the studio.
The studios also feared if the police department became aware of these women, they will lock them up on charge of vagrancy, since Hollywood's whores had no official residency in the city.
 In fact, when these extras were hired, their employment cards showed fake addresses given by the studios.
Orgies scenes were not something unconceivable.
They were shot in several films. For instance, the cost to shoot the Babylonian orgy sequence in "The Fall of Babylon" exceeded $200,000.
Cameraman Karl Brown talked about a scene, where actors and actresses playing the role of Babylonian harem were completely naked, and before filming that nudity scene, he was escorted out, because he was too young to see naked women, parading nude and doing all sorts of acts.
It is an absolute fact, that when Joseph Henabery was shooting several nudity scenes, producers and the studio's executives showed up on the set to remind him that the film needed more sex and 'frontal nudity" close-ups.
Even, the conservative Cecile B. DeMille shot obscene scenes and outrageous sex sequences; in his film "Manslaughter", 1922, we see a scene where two lesbians are kissing each other passionately, and their tongues inside each other' mouth.

Gloria Swanson wearing monkey fur.

Director Erich von Stroheim, a genius and a pervert.

So, it is very possible that von Stroheim's orgies scenes were shot indeed, and Gloria Swanson denied it for reasons we know and reasons we don't know.

In fact, it was Swanson who has suggested to von Stroheim to hire prostitutes for the orgies scenes. She poured a great deal of her own money in that film.

Thalberg himself complained about the huge number of extras (prostitutes,) von Stroheim hired for shooting those scenes, and the cost of those extravagant real embroidered underwear for the soldiers, and silk masks to cover the faces of extras who engaged in real kinky sex. Erich von Stroheim became famous for his sexual fetishes and orgies scenes in three films:

"The Wedding March", 1928,
"Merry-Go-Round", 1922,
"The Merry Widow", 1925.

Erich von Stroheim

Erich Von Stroheim (left) and Mae Busch (center) in a scene from the film "Foolish Wives," 1922.

Erich von Stroheim, (September 22, 1885 in Austria-May 12, 1957 in Seine-et-Oise, France.)
A director extraordinaire, a cinema legend...and a pervert. He was the first director to fully incorporate orgies scene and kinky sex in some of the most memorable films in the history of Hollywood, both "silents", and "talkies".
He fabricated a phantasmagoric story about his background, and claimed to be one of the aristocrats of Austria and Germany, while in reality, he came from a very modest family. He was the son of a lower-middle-class Jewish artisan.

From his quotes: "If you live in France and you have written one good book, or painted one good picture, or directed one outstanding film, 50 years ago, and nothing ever since, you are still recognized as an artist and honored accordingly.
In Hollywood, you're as good as your last picture. If you didn't have one in production in the last three months, you're forgotten, no matter what you have achieved."
His salary in Hollywood: $5,000 per week + 1,500,000 French Francs upon completion of the film Sunset Boulevard, 1950. In 1917, he got paid $75 a week.

*** *** ***

Louise Brooks "The Nymphomaniac Vampire."
(Nov. 14, 1906-Aug. 8, 1985)

Louise Brooks

Lots of ink and verses were poured into Hollywood chronicles of scandals, trashing people, jeopardizing careers, ruining marriages and families...and ironically, launching the careers of some. Sometimes, a scandal puts an end to star's career, but quite often, it catapults the rise of aspiring artists, starlets and stars. Scandal is a sword with a double-edge; either it cuts your throat, or breaks through impregnable barriers.

Louise Brooks

Some have used the casting couch, others, the influence of wealthy and powerful old *grand seigneurs* who were fond of young girls and soft silky skin.
In all cases, the actress and the diva in the making had to return the favors by engaging in sexual acts, and sharing partners, on the set, off the set, in the dressing room, even in wives' boudoirs. Sex, was their meal ticket.
Talent was not a prerequisite to start a career, rather, a dignified way to end it. Sinatra said: "Luck is 99% of the whole deal, talent comes much much later." In our scenario, sex is 99% of the whole deal, and luck is 1%. Many disagree.
But life is not always built upon objectivity, in Hollywood, subjectivity is a *force majeure*. Who fits this bill? Many.

And by many, I mean thousands of female stars who managed to shine, permanently or briefly. And the living examples abound, starting with Alla Nazimova, Theda Bara, Marion Davies, Jean Harlow, Joan Crawford, Clara Bow, and Louise Brooks.
But Louise Brooks is on the top of my list...for now.

*** *** ***

Sex was a game and a necessity to Brooks, and conjugal fidelity meant nothing to her.

Louise Brooks is unique.
An enigmatic character blended with sophistication, elegance, panache, intelligence, finesse, an exemplary loyalty to friends (But not to lovers or husbands!!), generosity, sarcasm, defiance, and insatiable sex appetite. And this appetite was disturbing quite a bit, because she could not function without having sexual partners around the clock.

A notorious, yet well respected French columnist, once said to me: "Louise c'est comme un ciseaux...il faut l'ouvrir pour que ca fonctionne." Translation: "Louise is like a pair of scissor. You got to open it to make it work." He meant that Louise had to spread her legs wide open to achieve what she has achieved on the screen and on stage. And Louise did! And quite often.
With his Parisian sarcasm, Jean Nohain once told me verbatim: "Every lover she had wanted to spend the rest of his life between her legs, but not a single minute as a wife." He meant, no one would trust her as a wife, because she was addicted to sex with multiple partners! Despite her scandalous affairs, Louise Brooks took Paris by storm, and the French adored her! C'est la vie!

Sex at fourteen!

"It is doubtful any film actress in the nineteen-twenties displayed a greater sense of overt sexuality on screen and off screen than Louise Brooks," said a commentator.
Louise's insatiable sex appetite, infidelity, and erotic curiosity got her into hot waters.

Louise Brooks

At fourteen, and as a nude model, she lost her virginity to a painter, who enjoyed her defloration with a number of other boys who were present at his studio. Louise Brooks did them all.
Willingly or unwillingly, sex maniac Louise Brooks inaugurated her sex life with a group sex! She admitted that event in her diary.
One year later, Louise was offered a small job in a touring dance troupe.
Two days later, Brooks began to sleep with the publicist of the troupe. Because of her obsession with sex, and constant demands for more sex, the publicist nicknamed her the "Hell Cat."
He begged for mercy, for Brooks has consumed all his physical energy, but Brooks kept on asking for more sex. Soon, gossip and rumors began to circulate about her nymphomania, and the multiple gang-bang sessions she had with the entire backstage crew. Brooks was fired.
Following the advice of a friend, Brooks moved to New York, looking for a job as dancer. She landed on the net of George White, who was notorious for producing risqué and nudity shows on Broadway. Worth mentioning here that White was arrested twice on charge of obscenity, and the district attorney shut down

(Twice) his show, and his vice squad arrested some of his female stars during the premiere. The same thing happened also to Earl Carroll, and to his "Vanities" show in 1924, and two of his female stars were booked for obscenity.
Welcome to the club, Dear Louise.

*** *** ***

Louise Brooks in New York: A call-girl with unorthodox habits and lots of sex.

In New York, Louise Brooks met the who's who of New York silky society. And her favorite men were the rich and powerful old ones. Ironically, Louise Brooks admitted that young men were far more exciting, but the older gentlemen procured her peace and stability.
She meant by stability, financial security, jewels, furs, diamonds and a ritzy apartment. And Louise got them all.

In her mind, being sexually active, and sharing multiple lovers, and sexual partners was not an immoral conduct, on the contrary, to Louise, sex was an effective way of communicating with others, inspirational, and even necessary for her creativity.
And working as an escort or a call girl did not offend her morality, as long as, she had the last word.
In New York, during the twenties and the thirties, it was customary in showbiz to throw elaborate parties for the "elder gentlemen" who poured their money in a show production. And parties meant, lots of skin, and lots of gorgeous stars and starlets solely invited to entertain the "dignitaries", and the aging angels. Simply put, Louise Brooks was both an artist and a sophisticated whore.
In her biography, Louise Brooks wrote: "In New York, there was a hand-picked group of beautiful girls who were invited to parties given for great men in finance and government. We had to be fairly well bred and of absolute integrity, never endangering the great men with threats of publicity or blackmail. At these parties we were not required, like common whores, to go to bed with any man who asked us, but if we did the profits were great. Money, jewels, mink coats, a film job, you name it."

In New York City, Louise Brooks stayed at the Algonquin Hotel. And Lord Beaverbrook picked up the tab. He was crazy about her. He covered her with jewels and gifts. Despite his generosity, Brooks never really cared about him.
In fact, she described him as an ugly monkey who had no manners. While the Lord was paying all her extravagant bills, Brooks was seeing a fleet of men.
A chambermaid described her room as a bordello.
The hotel management had no other choice than to kick her out. She moved to another hotel in Manhattan, and once again, she was asked to leave.

*** *** ***

From one man to another...constantly!

Because of her scandalous reputation, Brooks had to leave New York. People nicknamed her the "Nymphomaniac Vampire." Brooks settled for a while in Paris, where she took her audience and showbiz milieu by storm.
The French adored her.
She appealed to their taste; she was elegant, spoke French, and knew the French etiquette. In fact, she was well-read, and knew a lot about the French poets, Parisian literature, haute couture, and the pre-existentialist movement. Many thought she was French.

In Paris, Louise Brooks had multiple threesomes with the legendary French-Armenian photographer Demirjian, and high class prostitutes of his choice. A few months later, she received a telegram from Flo Ziegfeld, offering her a leading role in his extravagant "Follies." She packed up and returned to New York.
Brooks was well paid, but not well enough to carry on and maintain the standard of her debaucherie.
Prostitution and posing naked were added to her curriculum to cover her expenses and to support her outrageous life style.
She had a brief affair with Ziegfeld, but this "old rabbit" as she called him could not satisfy her. During one of her escapades, she met a multi-millionaire character by the name of John Lock. She moved into his ritzy apartment, and like Lord Beaverbrook, he showered her with diamonds and gifts.

Flo Ziegfeld.

But it was hard for Brooks to kick out her old nasty habit. She needed more men on a daily basis.
Lock caught her in the act with screenwriter Martin Townsend.
Lock went ape, when Louise asked him to undress and join in.
Lock kicked her out.

Brooks did not mind for a while, because a third man (Married with three children and a highly respected wife) was waiting for her.
Brooks moved in a third apartment fully paid by Martin. Mon Dieu, men never learn!
Martin was well connected.
He introduced her to Walter Wanger, who was in charge of shows production at the Players Lasky.
Martin regretted it later, when he learned that Brooks was sleeping with Walter Wanger.
How did she get the job?
Easy.

According to Nigel Cawthorne, "At the interview in his office, Wanger asked Louise what made her think she had what it took to make it in the movies. She took off her clothes, lay down on the couch and showed him."
Boom kaboom, Brooks got a contract, and moved with Wanger to Hollywood. So far, and in less than three months, Brooks had already slept with five men, in addition to several secret lovers.

*** *** ***

Louise Brooks in Hollywood: More sexual partners and lesbianism orgies.

Notorious lesbian, Peggy Fears, Louise Brooks' sexual partner in steamy orgies with Charlie Chaplin.

In Hollywood, Louise Brook's sexual appetite exploded. Her first two sexual partners were William Powell and Charlie Chaplin.
One of her most notorious affairs was her threesome with the "Little Rat" Charlie Chaplin (As she called him) and lesbian

Peggy Fears. During one of her multiple orgies with Peggy Fears, Louise Brooks met A. Blumenthal, a well-known figure of the motion pictures industry.

Brooks left Chaplin for Blumenthal, but occasionally, she would see Chaplin en cachette. But once she discovered that Chaplin had a venereal disease, Brooks dumped him for good.

Photos from L to R, Brooks' lovers: 1. Walter Wanger. 2. Lord Beaverbrook.

According to Cawthorne, "At the time, Chaplin was convinced that iodine prevented VD. One night at the Ambassador Hotel, he painted his entire genitalia and came charging at Louise and Peggy Fears with a bright red erection."

Brooks had enough of Charlie Chaplin and William Powell.

She began a new affair with director Eddie Sutherland, who was married at the time. They stayed together for two months, and got married.

Soon after, she fell madly in love with actor Buster Collier, who according to her diary, was the love of her life. While still dating Collier, behind the back of her husband, Brooks started a discreet affair with actress Constance Talmadge.

The woman is insatiable! Her infidelity and sex-mania did not stop here.

Louise Brooks with director/future husband Eddie Sutherland. She divorced in June 1928.

Now Louise Brooks began to experience a foursome. New sexual partners were added to her soupe du jour.

One of them was George Preston Marshall, owner of a chain of laundries and future owner of the Washington Redskins football team.

About him, Brooks said: "The most fateful encounter of my life." Then, something strange and very unusual happened. Brooks promised Marshall that she will be loyal to him, and she will

never again fool around. A promise, Brooks never gave to any of the 150 men she slept with. Well, that's promising.
But will Brooks keep her promise?
Far from it. A few days later, Brooks was found in bed with Greta Garbo.

George Preston Marshall, in front of the Red Skins office.

Marlene Dietrich heard about it and rushed to invite Brooks – allegedly to talk about Dimirjian—and the two ended digging into each other. "It was awesome," later on, Brooks will comment on her affair with Dietrich.

Rumors about her affairs with Greta Garbo and Dietrich began to circulate in Hollywood. The very graphic rumors caught the attention of another notorious lesbian, Pepi Lederer (Marion Davies' niece.) Well well!
What did happen to Brooks' promise to Marshall?
Gone with the wind, folks.

Lederer became Brooks' newest sexual partner.
Lederer was delighted, and she began to brag about her affair with Brooks. Jack Pickford was all ears.
He heard all the juicy details from Lederer.
This was a big mistake on the part of Lederer, because a few days later, she caught Brooks giving oral sex to Pickford! Worth mentioning here, that Louise Brooks was still married to Eddie Sutherland.

But this one was not an angel, either, for he was sleeping with several actresses, and an avalanche of Hollywood's beauties, including Bebe Daniels. The couple divorced, and Brooks returned to George Preston Marshall.
In 1933, she married Chicago millionaire Deering Davis, but abruptly left him in March 1934 after only five months of marriage, "without a good-bye... and leaving only a note of her intentions" behind her.
According to Card, Davis was just "another elegant, well-heeled admirer," nothing more.
The couple officially divorced in 1938, as reported by Squidoo.

One day, Clara Bow who also had an affair with Brooks, called her to let her know that George Marshall was fooling around. She advised her to get rid of him.
Bow suggested to Brooks, that she should focus her attention on Ben Schulberg, the big boss of Paramount. Brooks went to see Schulberg, a shrewd, tough cookie.
And as expected, Brooks spread her legs wide open, hoping that her sexual talent would do the trick. It did not.
Schulberg enjoyed the view, serviced the hungry slut, and promised to call her the very next morning. He never did.

Pepi Lederer.

The little we know about this obscure person came from a book written by Louise Brooks, titled "Lulu in Hollywood"; Brooks autobiography. In the book, Brooks reserved a whole chapter to Lederer. She was born Josephine Rose Lederer on March 18, 1910 in Chicago, Illinois.

Notorious lesbian, Pepi Lederer. (Marion Davies' niece.)

From L to R: Louise Brooks with the love of her life, Buster Collier, and Dorothy MacKaill, in a scene from the 1926 film "Just Another Blonde."

Facts about this most unusual woman:

Louise Brooks with John Wayne.

- After an unsuccessful attempt at operating a dance studio, she returned East and, after brief stints as a radio actor and a gossip columnist, worked as a salesgirl in a Saks Fifth Avenue store in New York City for a few years, then eked out a living as a courtesan with a few select wealthy men as clients.
- Brooks unfortunately had a life-long love of alcohol (more specifically gin), having begun drinking heavily at the age of fourteen and was an alcoholic for a major portion of her life.

- She was a notorious spendthrift for most of her life, even filing for bankruptcy once, but was kind and generous to her friends, almost to a fault.
- Despite her two marriages, she never had children, referring to herself as "Barren Brooks."
- Her many lovers from years before had included a young William S. Paley, the founder of CBS. According to Louise Brooks, Paley provided a small monthly stipend to Brooks for the rest of her life, and according to the documentary this stipend kept her from committing suicide at one point.
- George Marshall was the biggest reason she was able to secure a contract with Pabst. Marshall repeatedly asked her to marry him and after finding that she had had many affairs while they were together, married film actress Corinne Griffith instead.
- French film historians rediscovered her films in the early 1950s, proclaiming her as an actress who surpassed even Marlene Dietrich and Greta Garbo as a film icon (Henri Langlois: "There is no Garbo, there is no Dietrich, there is only Louise Brooks!"), much to her amusement.
- James Card, the film curator for the George Eastman House, discovered Louise living as a recluse in New York City, and persuaded her to move to Rochester, New York to be near the George Eastman House film collection. With his help, she became a noted film writer in her own right. A collection of her witty and cogent writings, "Lulu in Hollywood," was published in 1982.
- She rarely gave interviews, but had special relationships with John Kobal and Kevin Brownlow, the film historians, and they were able to capture on paper some of her amazing personality.
- She had lived alone by choice for many years, and Louise Brooks died from a heart attack in 1985, after suffering from arthritis and emphysema for many years.
- Brooks is considered one of the first naturalistic actors in film's history.
- She made her movie debut in 1925 for Paramount Pictures, and appeared in eleven films in less than three years starring opposite major stars such as W.C. Fields, and Adolphe Menjou.

- Brooks had always been very self-directed, even difficult, and was notorious for her salty language, which she didn't hesitate to use whenever she felt like it. In addition, she had made a vow to herself never to smile on stage unless she felt compelled to, and although the majority of her publicity photos show her with a neutral expression, she had a dazzling smile. By her own admission, she was a sexually liberated woman, not afraid to experiment, even posing fully nude for "art" photography, and her liaisons with many film people were legendary, although much of it is speculation.
- She described Garbo as masculine but a "charming and tender lover."
- She said: "When I am dead, I believe that film writers will fasten on the story that I am a lesbian. I have done lots to make it believable...All my women friends have been lesbians. But that is one point upon which I agree positively with Christopher Isherwood: There is no such thing as bisexuality. Ordinary people, although they may accommodate themselves for reason of whoring or marriage, are one-sexed. Out of curiosity, I had two affairs with girls - they did nothing for me."
- She was considered the most elegant star of the silent films era, and Hollywood golden age.
- She was one of the most photographed celebrities of her time.
- She was arrested in Kansas for lewd cohabitation. A term for adultery.
- She was kicked out of Kansas, flat broke.
- Went back to New York City and became the mistress of millionaire Sam Colt.
- Sam Colt got rid of her, because she continued to sleep with other men.
- Bisexual Tallulah Bankhead took her in. She sheltered her. And of course, the two became lovers.
- Bankhead got tired of her and asked her to leave her apartment. Brooks became a prostitute.
- She made no public apologies for preferring sex, and alcohol to a steady job.
- She said, "I have a gift for enraging people, but if I ever bore you, it'll be with a knife."

- She said, "I learned how to act by watching Martha Graham dance, and I learned how to dance by watching Charlie Chaplin act."
- About Berlin, Brooks wrote: "Sex was the business of the town. At the Eden Hotel, where I lived, the café bar was lined with the higher-priced trollops. The economy girls walked the street outside. On the corner stood the girls in boots, advertising flagellation. Actors' agents pimped for the ladies in luxury apartments in the Bavarian quarter. Racetrack touts at the Hoppegarten arranged orgies for groups of sportsmen. The nightclub Eldorado displayed an enticing line of homosexuals dressed as women. At the Maly, there was a choice of feminine or collar-and-tie lesbians."
- With a spate of popular Hollywood films under her belt including *The Show-Off* (1926), *A Girl In Every Port* (1928) and *Beggars Of Life* (1928), she thumbed her nose at Paramount and broke her contract to star in what would be her two greatest films, *Pandora's Box (Die Buchse der Pandora)* and *Diary of a Lost Girl (Das Tagebuch Einer Verlorenen)*, both with German director G. W. Pabst in 1929. These two films would elevate a good director to near-legendary status, make a cultural icon out of Brooks and virtually destroy the rest of her acting career in the process. Returning to Hollywood in 1931, she was relegated to supporting roles and B movies, before retiring in obscurity less than ten years later, as stated by David Jeffers.
- On August 8, 1985, Louise Brooks was found dead of a massive heart attack. She was buried in Holy Sepulchre Cemetery in Rochester, New York, as reported by Squidoo.

*** *** ***

Louise Brooks' lovers and sexual partners:

It was said that Brooks has slept with more than 150 men, and explored all sorts and types of sex, ranging from one night stand to group sex, and from straight sex to lesbianism. Among her most notorious sexual partners were (Just to name a few):

- A.C. Blumental.
- Alla Nazimova.
- Bebe Daniels.
- Ben Schulberg.
- Buster Collier.
- Charlie Chaplin.
- Clara Bow.
- Claudette Colbert.
- Constance Talmadge.
- Danny Aikman, a notorious nude model and bisexual.
- Deering Davis, a Chicago millionaire.
- Dimirhian, a French-Armenian photographer.
- Dorothy MacKaill.
- Dorothy Knapp.
- Earl Carroll.
- Eddie Sutherland (She married him).
- Fletcher Crandall, a crook.
- Flo Ziegfeld.
- George Preston Marshall.
- George W. Pabst, the German film-maker who took her under his wing in Germany, and launched her carrer in Europe. She was his mistress for 3 weeks. Then left him for Sepp Allgeier, his cameraman.
- George White.
- Gloria Swanson.
- Greta Garbo.
- Gustav Diessel, the German actor who co-starred with her in the Pandora Box. Louise played Lulu. In that film, Brooks and Diessel engaged into real sex. The film was banned in France and Germany for reason of obscenity. It contained real scenes of kinky sex, incest, and lesbianism.
- Humphrey Bogart.
- Jack Pickford.
- Jack Randall, a singing cowboy.
- James Card, a married man who was a photography curator at Kodak.
- James Dunne, a married Irish businessman in New York.

- Joan Crawford.
- John Kobal, a film historian.
- John Lock.
- John Wayne.
- Josephine Baker.
- Kevin Brownlow, a film historian.
- Lord Beaverbrook.
- Marlene Dietrich.
- Martin Townsend.
- Peggy Fears.
- Pepi Lederer.
- Rene Clair, French film-maker.
- Sam Colt, co-owner of the Colt guns company.
- Sepp Allgeier, a German cameraman.
- Tallulah Bankhead.
- Valeska Get, who introduced her to lesbians' orgies circles in Berlin.
- Walter Wanger.
- William Powell.
- William S. Paley, the founder of CBS.

George W. Pabst, the German film-maker who took her under his wing in Germany, and launched her career in Europe.

Scene from Earl Carroll's "Vanities", then...the most scandalous show in the country, starring Peggy Hopkins Joyce, then, the most notorious woman in America. Sophie Tucker, the "last of the red-hot Mommas," sang in the show. The show did not have household names, and no celebrated singers and performers. Without name recognition, Carroll had to feature nudity on a grand scale to sell tickets. Voila!

1924 Most Notorious Woman in America
Fantasy in the 1920s...vice squad...gorgeous girls...fabulous legs and delighted audience...

Earl Carroll's 1924 "Vanities" starring Peggy Hopkins Joyce, then the most notorious woman in America opened on September 10th and ran for 440 performances. It was the most scandalous show in the country, because nudity was a common element in "Vanities." The show catered to the so-called "busy and tired businessmen" by displaying "gorgeous legs", bared breasts, and parading 108 beautiful showgirls as peacocks at the sensual tempo of Ravel's "Bolero."

> Earl Carroll explained: "The aesthetic art of the number demands that the girls be in the absolute buff this time, not even G-strings."
> Leon Whipple in The Survey Magazine, March issue, 1926, described the show, its artists and performers, and the public reaction as follows: "For a not excessive price, men, women, and adolescents can go into a lovely New York theatre on Broadway and see naked bodies, generally of women, under full lights with nothing on save what antique writers call a "zone"(belt or girdle). The rest of the body is completely and absolutely nude, with scarce alleviation of a coat powder. The bodies are exposed as statues, figurines, and symbolic persons, with recurrent veilings and for brief flashes.

The showmanship is deft and even discreet though the shadowy lighting of yesteryear has given way to the full flood. The exposure of the body lasts probably five minutes out of the three hours, though there is a constant and cloying stream of lesser bareness — legs, backs, torsos, and anatomical odds and ends. To these latter we have already been acclimated for the unveiling has been going on in New York for several years, almost by fractions of inches as the producers tried out the public taste. Indeed, the student might find a thesis in social science in the scrutiny of this process of breaking down a convention by annual innovation. — Not Art and Not Model." (Source: Will A. Page, Behind the Curtains of the Broadway Beauty Trust, 1927)

Earl Carroll's "Vanities" show: Problem with the D.A., and New York Vice Squad!

New York City District Attorney did not like Carroll's decision. The New York Vice Squad was alerted. The next morning the D.A. demanded that Carroll should clothe the performers. Carroll refused. On September 11th, a police officer stood in the wings of the theatre ready to stop any nudity act, and brought with him several blankets.
The show opened with Kathryn Ray "in the buff" swinging upside down over an enormous clock. The officer rushed to the stage attempting to capture Ray and cover her with his blanket. But as agile as a rabbit, Ray broke free and vanished behind the stage. The audience thought it was part of the show!

Earl Carroll with his girls.

They loved this scene and applauded like maniacs. Meanwhile, the police officer was still chasing Kathryn Ray.

Two stagehands finally rescued Ray by getting her out of the theater from the stage back door.
The curtain fell, and the audience was still applauding! Short after, Earl Carroll stepped forward to tell the delighted audience, that the D.A. and the Board of Censors are trying to shut down his show.

Peggy Hopkins Joyce.

Born Marguerite Upton in 1893 to Berkley barber Sam Upton and his wife Dora Wood.
Peggy Joyce ran away from home in 1910 and rapidly she gained fame, and fortune, as Carroll's "stage nude performer", and later as Ziegfeld's showgirl. Later on, she became famous for her many marriages to millionaires.
She died in 1957.

The risqué and very controversial poster of Kathryn Ray.

The audience became furious and many of the "busy and tired businessmen" who were watching the show were indeed powerful and had connections in high places.
They assured Carroll that the show will go on. In fact, The Board of Censors lost its battle in a landslide *cause celebre,* and the show went on.
Kathryn Ray became a celebrity overnight.

The very next morning, waves of teenaged boys rushed to the lobby of the theatre to buy the poster of naked Kathryn Ray that was displayed in a prominent place in the lobby of the theater and strategically positioned to attract more people. And out of nowhere, the officer who tried once to catch Ray resurfaced again in the lobby, screaming and yelling at Carroll.
The police officer ordered him to remove Ray's huge poster. And as usual, Carroll refused. The furious policeman arrested Carroll on a charge of public obscenity.
Carroll found himself on trial on November 10, 1924 for displaying obscene posters.

The three judge panel of the Court of Special Sessions retired to consider their verdict which, they announced, would be based strictly upon the question of fact: Were the images immoral? "We have examined the exhibits that are specimens of nudity and find they are not sufficient to hold the defendant. We find the defendant should be acquitted."
W.C. Fields, who starred in several of Carroll's later revues, reached his own verdict: "Earl Carroll is a preacher with an erection." Lincoln Steffens might have found him an "honest crook." The premiere muckraking journalist of the Progressive Era, Steffens claimed to prefer "honest crooks," rascals who admitted their rascality so long as the admission could not be used against them in a court of law, over do-gooders of any sort. At least with an "honest crook" you got the truth.

Carroll began his statement to the judges by saying "I have always staked my name, my reputation, and when I had it, my money, on the conception of what people wanted to see."
He never pretended that the "Vanities" had any higher purpose than giving the audience what it craved.
This was, in a word, titilation."

Kathryn Ray was a stunning beauty.

Peggy Hopkins

Alice Fay

He won, and the show went on for another 438 performances. Meanwhile, and in many states in America, vice squads were cracking down on beauties bathing in revealing swimsuits...Women's beach suits were "censored!"
In that time in history, the great majority of young American women did not participate in a bathing beauty contest.
But thousands of them did go to beaches where their outfits and swimsuits raised the moral issues, Carroll faced.

*** *** ***

Faith Bacon

Faith Bacon was the most beautiful woman in the world (according to Florenz Ziegfeld) and the supposed inventor of the fan dance. When she was 20, Faith Bacon got a job in Broadway, as a chorus girl in Earl Carroll's *Vanities of 1930*. Carroll, a big time Broadway producer who, in his day, gloried in the snappy nickname, "the picker of pulchritude", was anxious to come up with a new way of getting some naked female flesh up on stage as part of the show.

In New York, it was legal to have nude women on stage as long as they didn't move, so shows often featured artistic tableaux with an array of stationary nudes.
However, that wasn't good enough for the pulchritude picker, who found himself in a creative crisis. There had to be a novel way of flashing some skin without getting arrested! At this moment of emergency, according to Faith's publicist -- clearly a fan of *42nd Street* (1933) -- "a chorine stepped out of line and offered a suggestion."
It was Faith, of course, taking a reckless chance to pitch her idea to the top man. "Mr. Carroll," she said, "Why can't we do a number where I'm covered when I move, and undraped when I stop? For example -- let's say the orchestra plays a waltz. I dance around, but on every third note, the music stops and I stand still and uncover!"
Carroll was impressed, and asked what she thought she could use to cover herself during the waltzing interludes. She suggested that ostrich feathers would be ideal, and so the fan dance -- truly, the zenith of American pre-war culture -- was born.

Protesting members from one of showman Earl Carroll's "Vanities" musical extravaganzas parade past Musician's Union Local 47's old headquarters. The Earl Carroll Theater on Sunset Boulevard presented classy risque dance productions performed by scantily clad women who were billed as "The Most Beautiful Girls in the World." In the 1938 dispute, Carroll complained the union was forcing his theater-restaurant to use a larger orchestra than was necessary. (L.A. Daily News)

Faith Bacon

A beach censor arresting two women in Chicago in 1922 for violating the laws concerning proper beach attire.

Faith toured America for the next few years, standing still on every third note, getting lots of ink in the gossip pages and occasionally getting busted by the police for outraging public decency, as mentioned in More than you need to know; King Feature Syndicate, 1938, and The Hammond Times, February 25 1937.

***   ***   ***

Sex, old men and gold diggers.

Just as Solomon could scarcely have "been very intimate" with most of his wives, the well-to-do New Yorker, or the anyone "above penury" who watched those naked women on stage, could not romance all one hundred or so beauties on stage at the Follies or the Vanities or Scandals.
An unlucky few "tired businessmen" fell for a particular girl.

Gilda Gray
One admirer of Gilda Gray, for example, tossed a diamond bracelet worth $100,000 onto the stage to show his appreciation.

Dorothy Knapp, another star of the Earl Carroll's show "Vanities" whom Carroll had billed as "the most beautiful girl in the world" and whose costume supplies a useful definition of what Page meant by the "minimum" worn by "the rest of the comely cast."

The most notable, because most unfortunate, was Stanley Joyce, Peggy Hopkins' third husband whose one-year marriage with the decade's most celebrated "gold digger" cost him at least two million dollars.

Indeed she entitled one chapter of her autobiography, *Men, Marriage, and Me* (1930) which described one week in her marriage to Joyce, "How to Spend a Million a Week." Will Page devoted several chapters of *Behind The Curtains* to stories of rich men taken for large sums by the "gold diggers" of the chorus.

According to Page, one admirer of Gilda Gray, for example, tossed a diamond bracelet worth $100,000 onto the stage to show his appreciation. Page, a press agent, quickly put the story in every newspaper he could. The incident, he related, made Gray a star, as reported by The Commodification of Fantasy in the 1920s.

*** *** ***

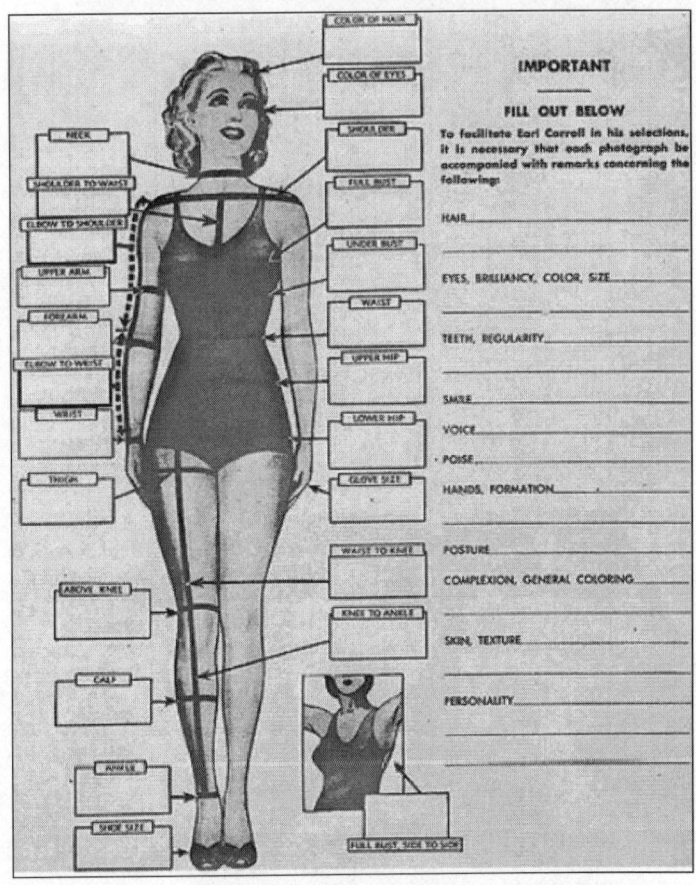

THE EARL CARROLL CHECK LIST
(5Ft, 5In, 118 Pounds were the magic numbers.)
All girls were required to fill out that application, and include information about their teeth, complexion and measurements! They were simply a piece of meat!

Mara Corday

Other Earl Carroll girls:
List, courtesy of Shirley Claire.

Dorothy Abbott,
Lois Andrews,
Barbara Jo Allen,
Eve Arden,
Lucille Ball,
Kitty Carlisle,
Shirley Claire,
Phyllis Coates,
Mara Corday,
Bette Davis,
Yvonne De Carlo,
Mary Eaton,
Dorothy Ford,
Jan Harrison,
Beverly Hecht,
Lola Jensen,
Ruby Lane,
Carole Lombard,
Marie MacDonald,
Marilyn Monroe,
June Nicholson,
Sheree North,
Gloria Pall,
Wanda Perry,
Lillian Roth,
Linda Stirling,
Lili St. Cyr,
Anya Taranda,
Caroline Tjulander,
Sophie Tucker,
Beryl Wallace.

The stunning and multi talented Shirley Claire is in the center.

Earl Carroll Girls' Reunion in Los Angeles, mid 1980's.
(Photo Credit: Shirley Claire)

Hollywood's Stars and Celebrities Who Slept with John F. Kennedy's

"JFK was pond scum." Wrote Newsweek, on August 19, 1996.

During the early 1960s, journalists and informed observers used to discuss in private the president's casual approach to his marriage vows, and his insatiable sexual appetite, but they nevertheless kept the code of silence that then protected the reputations of politicians (and those of the scribes as well). So Kennedy's extramarital affairs, and his dalliances with women on the fringe of organized crime, went unreported.

What the American people were allowed to see were carefully staged occasions, where Kennedy and his wife were seen at their best, displaying their sophistication and good taste. This was how, in the glow of network television, then at the height of its influence, the first truly glamorous presidential couple appeared before the nation. (Source: Professor Lewis L Gould)

In matters of sexual adventure, the Kennedy men have long gone in harm's way. Rose Kennedy's father, Boston Mayor John "Honey Fitz" Fitzgerald, was a known philanderer, but her mother bore it stoically.

Rose wished better for herself, but the pattern was replayed. Biographer Doris Kearns Goodwin, in The Fitzgeralds and the Kennedys, quotes a family member's recollection: "Even in the early years of their marriage, Joe had a reputation for being a ladies' man, and some of this gossip must have caught up with Rose."

As time passed, gossip was overtaken by flamboyant fact. Joe brought his women to his Palm Beach and Cape Cod estates and even took film star Gloria Swanson along with Rose on a voyage to Europe. Says Rose's former personal secretary Barbara Gibson: "She never showed any pain about those things."

Above all, according to author Garry Wills in The Kennedy Imprisonment, Rose took care "not to embarrass the men of the family, obstruct their careers, dim their accomplishments."

Rose gamely endured her husband's excesses, as did later generations of Kennedy women with the sons and grandsons who carried on the legacy of the founding father. Joe's sons reportedly used to provide their father with female companions when he visited them in Washington, D.C. During the '70s, Rose's grandsons Christopher Lawford and Joseph Kennedy II, as well as the then-married Teddy, would share daiquiris with young women at Rose's Palm Beach lunches, then head for the bedrooms after Rose retired for her nap, according to Gibson, interviewed recently by People magazine.

Jack was a chronic philanderer. Among his reported conquests were Angie Dickinson, Jayne Mansfield and Marilyn Monroe. Bobby also had an affair with Marilyn, as detailed in James Spada's soon to be released Peter Lawford: The Man Who Kept the Secrets. Ted carries on in the family tradition. The brothers' wives, Jackie and Ethel and Joan, had to live with the rumors as best they could. As though fated, Rose's daughters Pat and Jean ended up with faithless husbands as well.

Tolstoy was right, of course: Every unhappy family is unhappy in its own way—and no one can see into the real heart of another's family. Publicly and privately, all of the Kennedy women have had to find a way to cope. Some looked to the bottom of bottles, others upward to God.
Some triumphed, others failed. "The Kennedy men expect their sisters and wives to put up with everything as long as the fame and glory are pouring in," says an unkind friend of Jean Kennedy Smith's children who, like many people who discuss this powerful family, declines to be identified.
"The fathers set an example for the sons; the mothers set an example for the daughters. It will never cease..." as reported by Paula Chin, Joe Treen, Karen S. Schneider, People Magazine.

*** *** ***

List of names of Hollywood's stars and celebrities who had sexual intercourse with Kennedy:

- JFK did Lee Radziwill, Jackie's sister when Jackie was in hospital with Caroline.
- JFK did Audrey Hepburn.
- JFK did Jayne Mansfield for 3 years.
- JFK did Gene Tierney.
- JFK did Marlene Deitrich.
- Other actresses tied to JFK in the press were Kim Novak, Janet Leigh and Rhonda Flemming, but Fleming denied it.
- Angie Dickinson commenting on JFK's brutal lovemaking style called it "the best 20 seconds of my life."
- Jackie said JFK was a flop as a lover. She told a friend he "just goes too fast and falls asleep" as reported in the book "Grace and Power", by Sally Smith.
- During WWII, JFK was a security risk at the Pentagon for his well-known affair with Nazi spy Ingrid Arvad.
- In 1951, Kennedy had to pay off Alicia Purdom wife of a British actor half a million dollars after making her pregnant and then reneging on his promise to marry her.
- In 1956 Kennedy did Joan Lundberg who says he loved threesomes and was a voyeur. He paid for her abortion and slept with her in Jackie's marriage bed.
- 90 minutes before the first televised debate with Nixon, JFK was with a call-girl. (Reeves p 202) He also had a call-girl inauguration night. The night before the inauguration, he cheated on his wife in their Georgetown house.
- JFK kept an apartment at the Carroll Arms in Washington where he met young women. After a year of marriage a friend said of Jackie, "Jackie was wandering around looking like a survivor of an airplane crash." (Reeves p 116)
- JFK did Mary Pinchot Meyer in about thirty White House visits from Jan '62 to Nov '63. She was

mysteriously murdered in 1964 and her diary of their affair ended up at the CIA. Mary and JFK did drugs together.
- JFK did David Niven's wife.
- JFK did Pamela Turnure, 23, a Jackie look-a-like, hired as Jackie's press secretary, in an affair that went on three years in the White Hous JFK did Fiddle and Faddle, Secret Service code names for 21 and 23 year old staff members hired mostly for sex. JFK tested dangerous drugs on them without their knowledge by putting drugs in their drinks.
- White House intern Marion "Mimi" Beardsley whose married name is Fahnestock was 19 when JFK raped her (statutory rape - the age of consent was 21 in DC at the time). A powerful older man preying on vulnerable young women is what sexual harassment is all about.
- JFK got shots of speed from Dr. Max Jacobson, a.k.a. Dr. Feelgood.
- JFK had a penchant for swimming nude with his female guests at wild pool parties.
- JFK married socialite Durie Malcolm in Palm Springs in early 1947 and then a few days later had his friend Charles Spalding steal the marriage certificate from the Court House.
- JFK reportedly had an illegitimate child in the late 50s by prostitute Alicia Darr Clark who later tried to blackmail him.
- JFK did Judith Campbell Exner, mob moll, who had some twenty visits starting in May 1961. Exner carried cash bribes to JFK from California defense contractors. When she called JFK and told him that he had made her pregnant, he asked, "What are you going to do about it?" She had an abortion at a Chicago hospital in January 1963. She was never invited back to the White House. Her lover, mob boss Sam Giancana, bragged that he had 'placed' her with the President. Interestingly, both Giancana and another of her mob lovers, Roselli, were given the C.I.A. contract to kill Castro.
- JFK did Ellen Rometsch, an East German spy. When the Profumo affair (a sex scandal with a German spy) was blowing apart the British government, the Kennedys

paid her off and had her deported. They abused both the FBI and Congress (by threatening Congressmen with information from their FBI files) to keep this liaison out of the press and the timing strongly suggests that the assassination of South Vietnam's Diem was used to divert press attention from JFK's connection to Rometsch. Kennedy also had had sex both in London and New York with prostitute Suzy Chang who was at the heart of the Profumo affair. Bobby had a hard time covering this up.

- When the Secret Service was asked by local officials in Seattle if Kennedy always had prostitutes brought to him, they answered, "We travel during the day, so this only happens at night." Truckloads of prostitutes were brought to the Whitehouse and admitted without security checks. When JFK inspected military bases, he expected to be supplied with women.
- JFK used Peter Lawford's home in Santa Monica for meeting women.
- JFK kept a large collection of photos of himself with naked women.
- When President, Kennedy blackmailed starlets into servicing him or have their careers destroyed.
- JFK suffered from permanent venereal disease because he had been re-infected so often. He infected his partners with a disease so serious that it causes 35 percent of all infertility in US women.
- Marilyn Monroe told a columnist that JFK would not indulge in foreplay because he lacked the time. They had a one-year affair. Bobby Kennedy also did her and she even aborted his baby which, if she told, would have destroyed his career. The day Monroe died, neighbors saw Robert F. Kennedy and "a man with a doctor's bag" together enter her house. Within four hours she was found dead. Monroe was killed with a barbiturate suppository, but a bottle of oral pills was left at the scene to make it look like a possible suicide. U.S. Attorney General Kennedy was never questioned about his role and his cousin actor Peter Lawford who "cleaned up" the murder scene never explained what happened to Marilyn's incriminating diary.

- The Kennedys were banned from the funeral. JFK is quoted by Traphes Bryant as saying to a friend, "I'm not through with a girl till I've had her three ways." (Reeves p 241).
- During a 1961 meeting in Bermuda with British Prime Minister Harold McMillian Kennedy said, "I wonder how it is with you, Harold? If I don't have a woman for three days, I get terrible headaches." There is a much more vulgar Kennedy quote along the same line in Hersh page 389, as reported on JFK Scandal Page.

*** *** ***

Janet Leigh

Mary Pinchot Meyer

A new book, *John F. Kennedy: A Biography* by Michael O'Brien (St. Martin's Press, NYC 2006) describes briefly an affair JFK had with Mary Pinchot Meyer, the former wife of CIA agent Cord Meyer and sister of Washington Post editor Ben Bradlee's wife Tony. It says, "On the evening of July 16, 1962, according to [Washington Post executive] Jim Truitt, Kennedy and Mary Meyer smoked marijuana together.

The White House was hosting a conference on narcotics in two months, and Kennedy joked about it to Mary. (Truitt claimed he himself provided Mary with the pot.) The president smoked three of the six joints Mary brought to him. At first he felt no effects. Then he closed his eyes and refused a fourth joint. 'Suppose the Russians did something now,' he said. Kennedy allegedly told Mary that the pot 'Isn't like cocaine,' and informed her that he would get her some cocaine."

O'Brien notes that during her affair with Kennedy, Meyer visited Timothy Leary, a fact confirmed in Robert Greenfield's fairly comprehensive new book, *Timothy Leary: A Biography* (2006, Harcourt), published on the 10th anniversary of Leary's death. Leary wrote in *Flashbacks* that Meyer told him she wanted to run an LSD session with a famous public figure, and after Meyer was found murdered in October 1964, Leary theorized it was JFK and that she'd recorded the event in her diary, which was never found. Sources: Very Important Pothead; The Washington Post.

Mary Pinchot Meyer.

Less than a year after President John F. Kennedy was assassinated in Dallas, his favorite Washington mistress—Mary Pinchot Meyer—was shot dead, execution-style, just a short distance from her home in the safest part of D.C.'s safest neighborhood. Meyer was a stunning blonde and a free-spirited Georgetown artist.
A pre-hippie hippie, she was a smart Vassar grad, a former reporter for United Press, a socialist/pacifist, and a sexual adventurer who also experimented with mind-altering drugs.

The CIA had been able to keep close tabs on Mary's nearly two-year affair with President Kennedy—partly because the spy agency, it was later revealed, had been bugging her home and telephones ever since her late-'50s divorce from Cord Meyer, a top CIA official.
According to Nina Burleigh, author of *A Very Private Woman*, the bugs were ordered by CIA counterintelligence chief James Jesus Angleton, a strange-looking, heavy-drinking Cold Warrior whose specialties were illegal break-ins (other spooks called him

"the Locksmith") and searching for Soviet moles within the agency.

Angleton had socialized with the Meyers while they were married and continued to be friendly with both. (Burleigh's information about the bugging came from an interview she did with Joan Bross, the wife of John Bross, a high-ranking CIA official.) Report by D. Fulsom.

*** *** ***

Alicia Purdom

Alicia Purdom, estranged wife of actor Edmund Purdom, seen with her lawyer, Avvacato Giuliani, at the Palace of Justice. (Bettman)

Ellen Rometsch, an East German spy.

Had the American public known in 1963 what they know now about John F. Kennedy's scores of sexual escapades, would he have been able to survive in office? Though he was charismatic and capable, probably not. Particularly if it were known that one of the President's girl friends was—as is now reputed—a White House intern.

Carroll Arms

JFK kept an apartment at the Carroll Arms in Washington where he met young women.

And even more especially, if it were known that one of his bedmates were a prostitute and a reputed Soviet Bloc spy.

The intern, Mimi Beardsley Alford, then 19 and now 66, is penning a memoir—*Once Upon a Secret*—that claims she had an affair with President Kennedy from June 1962 to November 1963. Sources: Don Fulsom, Crime Magazine.

***   ***   ***

Durie Malcolm

Durie Malcolm (1917-2008) at age18.   Durie Malcolm circa 1960.

Jack Kennedy married Durie Malcolm—a twice divorced Palm Beach socialite in 1947. Joe Kennedy was FURIOUS. He planned on running his son for the Presidency and a divorcée was not Presidential timber.
He had the marriage annulled, but a formal civil divorce was never obtained. Kennedy Senior was FURIOUS when he heard about the marriage.

At that time, a divorced man—no matter how rich—had absolutely no chance of making it to the White House. Nelson Rockefeller—whose family *owned* the United States—knew that all too well.
Joe Kennedy had all traces of the marriage removed, and Durie was offered a substantial sum to buy her silence....As a further COVER-UP, she was quickly married in New Jersey to a Thomas Shelvin in July of that same year. Reported by Niall Kilkenny.

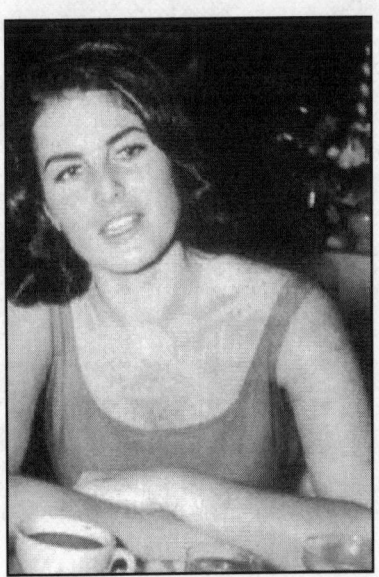

Judith Exner, Momo's Moll, Frank Sinatra introduced her to JFK.

Jackie Kennedy and Lee Radziwill by John F. Kennedy Casket, 1968. Kennedy did Lee Radziwill.

Inga Arvad. Nazi Spy, FBI recorded her romps with Ensign JFK.

Patricia Bowman

Ellen Rometsch

John Kennedy's lover, Judith Campbell Exner, who was a direct link to the Mafia.

Sam Giancana (second from right), mob boss of Chicago, with the Mcguire sisters, also a target of the Kennedy's after first being helped by him to win the elections in Illinois, felt betrayed by the Kennedy's. He sent his hitmen to Dealey Plaza, among others Charles Nicoletti and Johnny Roselli. All three were murdered in the 1970's shortly before they were called to testify before government committees investigating the murders of JFK and Martin Luther King. Charles Nicoletti was James Files' boss.

Exner: "I was crucified because I had had the audacity to have an affair with Jack Kennedy."

Mariella Novotny being taken into custody by the FBI.

Kennedy, his sex addiction, and national security.
The President who slept with whores, Mafia's women, and Russian spies!

In the Sydney Morning Herald, July 20, 2007 , reporter Jodie Pfarr wrote (Verbatim, and unedited): The sexual shenanigans of John Fitzgerald Kennedy sure put the antics of Bill Clinton and Monica Lewinsky into perspective.

This tell-all (or is it?) documentary exposing JFK's own dirty laundry reveals a man prepared to risk his country's security for a shag. But back in the '60s, public life was public knowledge and private life remained just that. So who can blame him for taking advantage, especially a man of his needs?

Judith Campbell

Spokeswoman for the first lady, Pamela Turnure in 1963. Turnure was one John F. Kennedy many lovers, and sexual partners.

Gallery of stars and celebrities who slept with John F. Kennedy, to name a few:

Jayne Mansfield; he did her for 3 years.

Audrey Hepburn

Kim Novak?

Gene Tierney

Marlene Dietrich

Nazi spy Ingrid Arvad.

Angie Dickinson

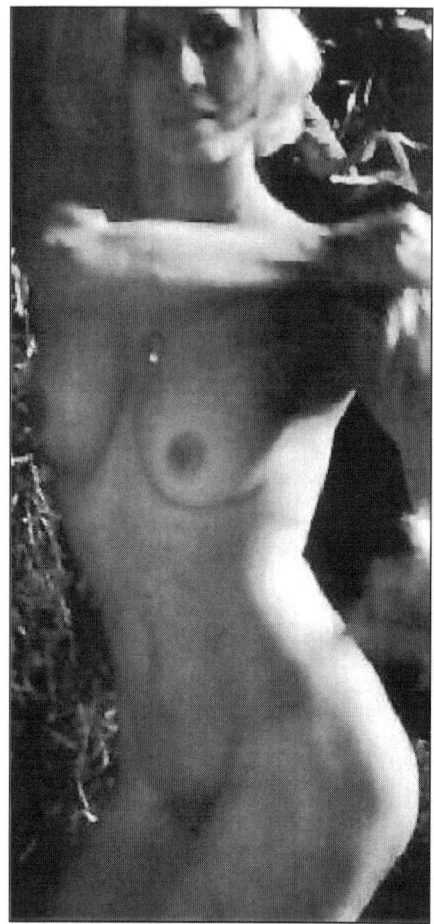

Angie Dickinson, commenting on JFK's brutal lovemaking style called it "the best 20 seconds of my life."

Mary Pinchot Meyer (Far right), who was mysteriously murdered in 1964 and her diary of their affair ended up at the CIA. Mary and JFK did drugs together.

Mrs. Hjordis Niven, David Niven's wife.
Kennedy did her as well.

John Kennedy slept with 26 actresses; stars, starlets and celebrities, the most famous ones (to name a few):
- Mary Biib,
- Ellen Romesch,
- Marilyn Monroe,
- Mary Meyer,
- Judith Exner,
- Angie Dickinson (commenting on JFK's brutal lovemaking style, Dickinson called it "the best 20 seconds of my life.")
- Audrey Hepburn,
- Gene Tierney,
- Jayne Mansfield,
- Marlene Deitrich,
- Janet Leigh,
- Hjordis Niven, David Niven's wife.

And those who procured him the goodies, (to name a few) were: Frank Sinatra and Peter Lawford.

Peter Lawford

Frank Sinatra

Jayne Mansfield. John F. Kennedy did her for 3 years. (From Owens Archives)

Mansfield and Tommy Noonan in the most repeated nude scene of the movie Promises! Promises!

Jayne Mansfield as a stripper!

Jayne Mansfield ended her career as she began: posing nude and working as a stripper. This reminds me of Madonna, who started as a nude model for several years after she first moved to NYC in 1979.

She would became famous for posing nude during the first half of the 1990s and especially in December 1992 with the release of her book, SEX. Madonna is now back at it again as the cover of the latest February 2002 *Pop* magazine revealed.

Madonna, like Jayne Mansfield to the very end, continues to capitalize on her valuable natural endowments.

*** *** ***

Mary Astor's Diary: Sex and lust...lovers and multiple orgasms...

This picture is from the 1936 trial over the custody of Marilyn Astor Thorpe.

Mary Astor charged that her ex-husband, Franklyn, wasn't a fit parent (he allegedly had women spend the night while his daughter was in his custody and was supposedly abusive to the girl) and he made similar accusations; citing passages in her diary describing her affair with playwright George S. Kaufman. From left, Attorney Joseph Anderson, Franklyn Thorpe, attorney Ethel M. Pepin (that's the lady in the hat), attorney A.P. Michael Narlian, attorney Roland Rich Woolley and Mary Astor. Ruth Chatterton is in the audience between Thorpe and Pepin.

This piece is taken from my book "Hollywood Earth Shattering Scandals"

In her diary, Mary Astor had a list of her lovers, including the principal player, George Kaufman, and Gene Fowler, who was at the top of the list of her skilled lovers, and "Fuckers"; a term, Astor used in her diary.
Allegedly, 16 lovers featured in the diary, and largely detailed host sex scenes and encounters were described. Astor's diary was so erotic, and so extremely sexually charged, which made the judge presiding over her trial, confiscate the diary, and later ordered to be incinerated.
Astor's diary earned her the infamous reputation of being "The greatest nympho-courtesan since Madame Pompadour."

*** *** ***

Juicy erotic excerpts from Astor's diary describing her extramarital affairs and love-making. In her own words and writing:

- "Sexually I was out of control."
- "Ah desert night with George's body plunging into mine, naked under the stars..."
- "We played kneessies during the first two acts, my hand wasn't in my own lap during the third...It's been years since I've felt up a man in public, but I just got carried away..."
- "His (George Kaufmann) powers of recuperation are amazing, and we made love all night long...and we shared our fourth climax at dawn..."
- "He went down on me, and I exploded..."
- "Was any woman ever happier? It seems that George is just hard all the time...I don't see how he does it, he is perfect."
- "He tore out of his pajama and I never was undressed by anyone so fast in all my life."
- "It was wonderful to fuck the entire sweet afternoon away...I left about 6 o'clock."

Her most famous sexual partners were (To name a few):

1. John Barrymore,
2. Humphrey Bogart,
3. Gordon Wheelock,
4. Manuel Campo,
5. George Kaufman,
6. Gene Fowler.

One would assume that these revelations would destroy an actress' career, but they did not, far from it. Au contraire mon cher ami, au contraire, Mary Astor scored high on the chart of fame and success. She became one of Hollywood's most bankable stars after the scandal.
C'est la vie, Hollywood has a double-standard!

Previously, Mary Astor had many many steamy sexual affairs with Hollywood's leading men, like Humphrey Bogart, and the sex-maniac John Barrymore who deflored her at the age of 17 in his dressing room.
The decadent Barrymore taught her how to please a man at multiple levels. He told his friends how fascinated he was with her "sexual naivete."

But Astor grew up to become an expert in sex and extra-marrital affairs. But her husband, Dr. Franklyn Thorpe was not a saint either. He fooled around quite a bit; his favorite dish was young and stupid starlets like Norma Taylor, and his greatest satisfaction came from threesome with the "Bathing Beauties", and Busby Berkeley showgirls, and those who were called "Extras", then, another word for Hollywood harem and beautiful girls hired by studios for sexual acts and orgies scenes; hores! The master of these orgies ceremonies was none but Erich von Stroheim.

*** *** ***

Rare photo of Mary Astor.

Greta Garbo and John Barrymore, in "Grand Hotel", 1932.

John Barrymore was on the list of Mary Astor's most famous lovers. He deflored her at the age of 17 in his dressing room.

Humphrey Bogart and Mary Astor in "The Maltese Falcon," 1941
Warner Bros.

Humphrey Bogart had a brief but steamy sexual relationship with Mary Astor. He told his friends how insatiable and stupid Astor was.

George Kaufman's headlines were more usually found in the drama reviews for plays like The *Band Wagon, Dinner at Eight, The Man Who Came to Dinner, Night at the Opera*, and others of the more than 60 he eventually wrote alone or with collaborators; or for first-run Broadway plays that he directed, like *My Sister Eileen, Front Page, Of Mice and Men*, and *Guys and Dolls*. (Lacy Conradt)

George S. Kaufman, the principal lover of Mary Astor.

Original caption: 8/15/1936-New York, NY: Confessing that he lost seven pounds while the famous "misstep diary" of Mary Astor was being read in the recent custody suit in Los Angeles.

TUESDAY MORNING.

AFFAIR WITH PLAYWRIGHT ADMITTED BY MARY ASTOR

Actress Asserts Spouse Condoned; Judge Calls for Her Diary; Barrymore Subpoena Due

Associations with George S. Kaufman, which were condoned by her husband, Dr. Franklyn Thorpe, were admitted on the witness stand yesterday by Mary Astor, screen actress, in the sensational battle between mother and father for their 4-year-old child, Marilyn.

That, coupled with disclosure that most of the 200 pages of intimate secrets concerning Miss Astor's private life, written painstakingly in lavender ink by the actress in her diary, have mysteriously disappeared, was the principal evidence adduced at the close of yesterday's sessions of the trial.

SAYS MATE AWARE

That Dr. Thorpe was aware of this affair between the red-haired screen actress and the Broadway playwright six months before he filed suit for divorce, and that during those six months Mary Astor and Dr. Thorpe lived together as man and wife, was declared by Miss Astor under the cross-examination of Attorney Joseph Anderson.

"You know George Kaufman has nothing to do with this divorce," Miss Astor said she told her husband at the time he brought the divorce action. "You've known about him since last September (1934) and you've condoned it. Now you bring it up in order to threaten me and obtain the custody of my baby."

the actress said she knew her husband wanted to "shame" her.

At least a month before Dr. Thorpe is said to have threatened her, Miss Astor said she had consulted an attorney about a divorce.

"I did wish to be free from Dr. Thorpe because of his constant association with Lillian Miles," she blurted before Attorney Anderson could stop the witness.

But at that time she did not know that her former husband intended to put up a fight for baby Marilyn and name Kaufman in the action.

As for the divorce action, she repeated again and again that she had instructed her attorney to do exactly as Dr. Thorpe ordered.

CHARGES THREAT

"He said he would blacken my name," declared the actress, "plaster my name and that of my prominent friends over the front pages of every paper in the country, wreck and ruin my career as an actress. I told him it was a horrible thing to do and that, if he wrecked my career I wouldn't be able to earn money for my child's care— a thing which he can't or won't do."

The screen player was accompanied to court by Ruth Chatterton, also dressed in white, and by Miss

Headlines in the newspapers.

Mary Astor with her child.

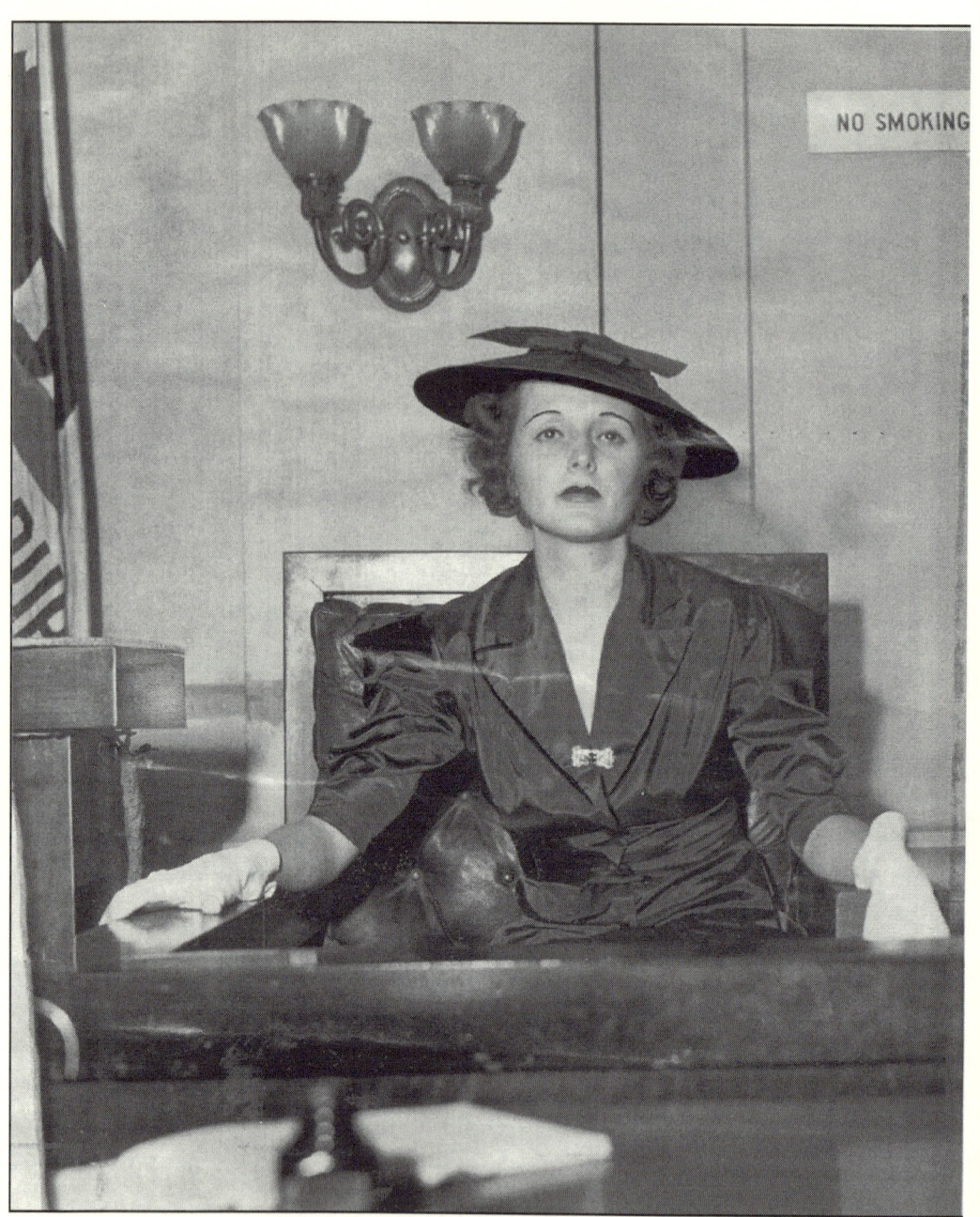

Mary Astor in court.

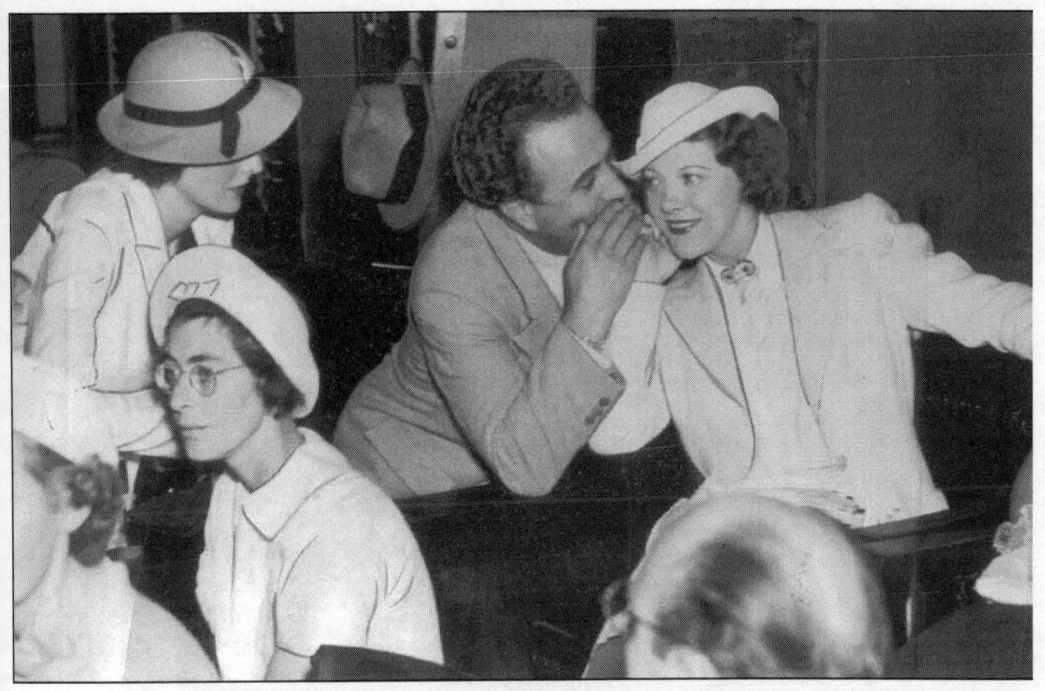
Mary Astor, Roland Richard Woolley and Ruth Chatterton.

> 113
>
> frequently to 73rd Street. I remember one morning about 4 we had a sandwich at Reubens and it was just getting daylight so we drove through the park in an open cab and the street lights went out and the birds started singing and it was cool and dewy and pretty heavenly. The evening I left we had dinner at Twenty-One and a bottle of lovely wine — he had a car and drove me to the airport kissed me good-bye. ~~~~~~~~~~~~~~~
>
> Monday January 15th
>
> That was six months ago and it's still good — we write to each other often; about every two weeks — flowers and telegrams for Xmas & New Year's — once when Franklyn was away on a hunting trip he called me long distance and we talked for half an hour — his last letter finished with Think of me, my darling, because I certainly think of you. If it's

A page from Mary Astor's diary, written in lavender ink.

Mary Astor's most famous dates and assumed lovers
(To name a few)

Howard Hughes
Douglas Fairbanks
Ben Lyon
Clark Gable
Gene Fowler
John Houston
John Saunders
David Dalton
Ronald Colman
Irving Asher
Joseph Taylor
Dr. Franklyn Thorpe
Thomas Gordon

Howard Hughes   Gene Fowler   Douglas Fairbanks

John Houston

Ben Lyon   John Saunders   Ronald Colman

Dr. Franklyn Thorpe

The "Sewing Circle" Concept
Hollywood's gay/bisexual actresses, 1920's to 1950's

The "Sewing circles"
The term "Sewing circles," is allegedly coined by actress Alla Nazimova to describe discreet gatherings of Hollywood lesbians; it became a common way of referring to lesbian and bisexual actresses of that era. Many actresses of the 1930s, 1940s, and 1950s participated in the "sewing circles."
They lived double lives.
It was during this time that 'lavender marriages' became common. 'Lavender marriages' gave the public appearance of famous people being married, while in private they shared separate lives, having lovers of the same sex as either their significant other or temporary affair. (Data: Hollywood's Golden Age of Lesbianism. The Examiner, Atlanta, Leslie Davis.)

Many were lesbian, including (To name a few):
- 1. Alla Nazimova,
- 2. Greta Garbo,
- 3. Eva Le Gallienne,
- 4. Pepi Lederer,
- 5. Patsy Kelly,
- 6. Jean Acker,
- 7. Judith Anderson,
- 8. Katharine Cornell,
- 9. Lizabeth Scott,
- 10. Agnes Moorehead.

Others were bisexual, including (To name a few):
- 1. Tallulah Bankhead,
- 2. Laurette Taylor,
- 3. Louise Brooks,
- 4. Peggy Fears,
- 5. Marlene Dietrich,
- 6. Joan Crawford,

- 7. Beatrice Lillie,
- 8. Barbara Stanwyck (Had numerous affairs with Marlene Dietrich and Joan Crawford)
- 9. Claudette Colbert,
- 10. Clara Bow,
- 11. Janet Gaynor,
- 12. Pola Negri,
- 13. Lili Damita, the former wife of Errol Flynn, with whom, she had a stormy marriage.
- 14. Winifred Rennie.

*** *** ***

Sybil Thorndike

Alla Nazimova's bisexuality was common knowledge in the film community despite her long-term involvement with gay actor Charles Bryant.

Nazimova was notorious for her lavish parties, which were rumored to involve "debauched sexual acts involving women" (no telling what the FBI defined as debauched in those days).

Nazimova's relationships with writer Mercedes de Acosta, stage actress Eva Le Gallienne, film director Dorothy Arzner and Oscar Wilde's niece Dolly earned her a reputation as a bit of a "player." Nazimova, with lesbian notoriety, became known as "unsafe" in Hollywood.

She was effectively blacklisted.

Many lesbian actresses retreated deeply into the closet, dating or marrying men in order to appear heterosexual.

Patsy Kelly with Basil Rathbone.

Lily Damita

Being 'out' was career suicide.

Yet several actresses in the decades to follow, such as the seductress Marlene Dietrich and the irrepressible Tallulah Bankhead, appeared unconcerned about the gossip surrounding their sexuality.

They encouraged it. Bankhead consistently made quips alluding to her lesbianism. She had a long term relationship with one of the only openly lesbian actresses of the time, comedienne Patsy Kelly. However, she adored Garbo and pursued her relentlessly, which seems to have worked because she reportedly had affairs with Greta Garbo and Marlene Dietrich.

Tallulah participated in the 'sewing circles.' While in Hollywood, she was often a guest at Nazimova's 'Garden of Alla.' (Data: Hollywood's Golden Age of Lesbianism. The Examiner, Atlanta, Leslie Davis. Flickr.)

Her lesbian partners included:
- Katharine Cornell,
- Laurette Taylor, also a lover of Nazimova and director Dorothy Arzner,
- Sybil Thorndike,
- Beatrice Lillie. Lillie had affairs with Eva Le Gallienne, Cornell and Judith Anderson. It just gets so confusing.

Winifred Rennie (left) and Patsy Kelly.

Director Dorothy Arzner.
She slept with an avalanche of ingénues, starlets and major stars (actresses, of course.)

Judith Anderson
A major star of the era, as well as a lesbienne.

Claudette Colbert, a notorious bi-sexual, and member of the Sewing Circle.

Eva Le Gallienne

Eva Le Gallienne.
She was a very exceptional woman.
Talented, and highly cultured. Eva Le Gallienne was born in London in 1899, the daughter of Julie and Richard le Gallienne. She came to New York with her mother when she was 18. In New York, she directed and produced several plays. Always a lesbian, Eva never married, instead she took many lovers from the "Sewing Circle", and the art community in Manhattan. She lived all her life with lesbians, and occasionally, she would welcome gay men. Her first lovers were Mercedes de Acosta, Greta Garbo and Alla Nazimova.

Alla Nazimova's "Garden of Allah", the Mecca of lesbianism, bisexuality and orgies.

The official center of the "Sewing Circle", where hundreds upon hundreds of lesbians and bisexuals would spend long weekends screwing and pampering each other, usually at the tempo of a band of musicians made from "neutered boys" from Ethiopia, who served the demanding participants with all sorts of fetish and repulsive sexual acts, mainly disgusting anal sex and oral sex!!
The majority of Hollywood stars and big shot actresses of the era were nothing more than the scum of the earth!

In 1979, at the age of 80, Eva went to Hollywood to make a film "Resurrection." She wrote in her diary: "I just looked out of the window onto Sunset Boulevard and the ceaseless flow of traffic. It is 10 at night. The tremendous stretch of this quiet road - so unreal. In my thoughts, as I look across the road, I see Alla's house as it was in 1921.

Then, it was the last house in Hollywood. Beyond it wild country. Her lovely garden filled with orange, lemon and grapefruit. All enclosed - all very private - and so quiet.

Another life, another world. I'm so glad to have known it. I pity the young people who only know the world as it is now. It is well worth being 80 to have known that other one. What a wonderful life I have had! How grateful I am for it."

At one time, Eva took Broadway by storm when she played the role of Peter Pan.

Eva was a chart-member of the "Sewing Circle", originally created by Nazimova, and funded for a while by Pola Negri. It was heard (But never substantiated) that Eva wrote a special piece of music for Nazimova's orgies sessions at Nazimova's residence/hotel, known as the "Garden of Alla." The musicians who played the piece were all Black gays from Ethiopia.

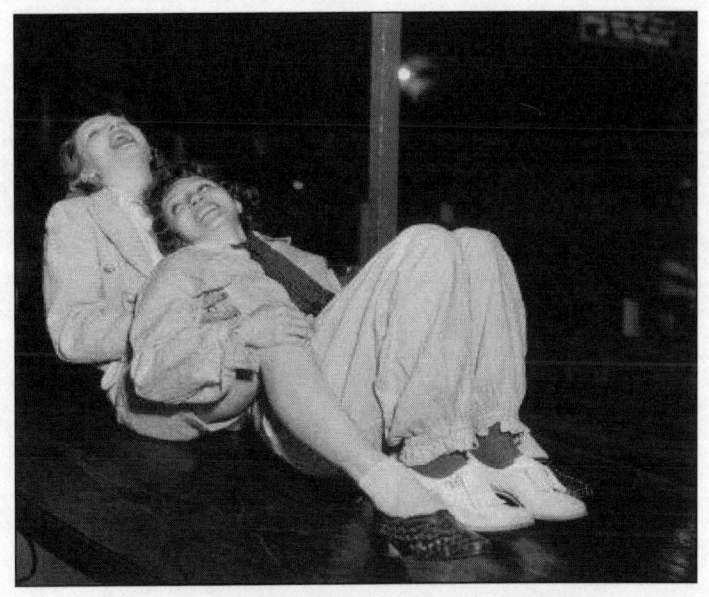

Claudette Colbert and her lover Marlene Dietrich.

Mercedes de Acosta, the "Female Lover of the Stars".
Brooks: "She screwed everybody in town..."
Photograph of the older Mercedes, taken by her lover Marlene Dietrich.

> **Orgies with de Acosta, Greta Garbo, Irving Thalberg, Hope Williams, Tallulah Bankhead, Bessie Marbury, and Eleonora von Mendelssohn.**

From a letter written by Alice B. Toklas to Anita Loos in 1960: ".....you can't dispose of Mercedes lightly; she has had the two most important women in the US, Greta Garbo and Marlene Dietrich...and well known women and men in the literary and artistic planes of both New York and Hollywood." As mentioned in Biography: Here Lies The Heart, 1960.

Mercedes met Greta Garbo for the first time at the residence of the Ukrainian writer, Salka Viertel (Lover of Garbo and Berthold Viertel) who persuaded Irving Thalberg to consider Garbo for "Queen Christina."
Garbo and de Acosta had an orgy with Thalberg.

Further encounters will include:
- Hope Williams,
- Tallulah Bankhead,
- Bessie Marbury,
- Eleonora von Mendelssohn, notorious for her bisexuality.

They all met in New York at Tallulah's apartment.

De Acosta was one of the prominent figures of her circle, yet, there is no biography of her. However, she was featured in Greta Garbo and Marlene Dietrich biographies. Mercedes was reluctant to publish her own. She thought that her biography would be either censored or misunderstood.

*** *** ***

Bessie Marbury

Marbury joined the Sewing Club very discreetly, and even though she had multiple sexual encounters with Greta Garbo, da Costa and Thalberb, she continued a well-known lesbian relationship with Ella de Wolf.
Her affairs well very-well known in Hollywood, and surely made headlines in the media and entertainment milieu. As a matter of fact, her lesbianism was reported by the New York Times.
When Ella Anderson de Wolfe got married to Sir Charles Mendl, on March 10, 1926, the New York Times wrote about her marriage on page one: "The intended marriage comes as a great surprise to her friends..."
Why?
Because everybody knew about her lesbian relationship with Elizabeth Marbury, who had numerous sexual relations with an avalanche of actresses.
Since 1892, de Wolf and Marbury were openly living together as lovers. The New York Times added, "When in New York she makes her home with Miss Elizabeth Marbury at 13 Sutton Place."
New York society called de Wolfe and Marbury "The Bachelors."

Gossipers rushed to say that Elsie married the English diplomat and aristocrat for the title. And many believed that the marriage was never consumed. Elizabeth Marbury and de Wolfe continued their affair behind closed doors, until Marbury's death in 1933.

Ella Anderson de Wolfe (Lady Mendl), sexual partner and lover of Bessie Marbury for years.

Young Ella Anderson de Wolfe.

Eva Le Gallienne as Peter Pan.
Her early lovers were Mercedes
de Acosta and Alla Nazimova.

Greta Garbo with Ukrainian writer Salka Steuermann Viertel.
It was Viertel (Lover of Garbo and Berthold Viertel) who persuaded Irving Thalberg to consider Garbo for "Queen Christina."

> **Mercedes and her relationship with Marlene Dietrich, and Greta Garbo.**
> Mercedes' friendship/affair with Marlene Dietrich differs greatly from Maria Riva's version in Marlene Dietrich by her daughter; and there is evidence in letters to back up the Dietrich camp's rather disdainful estimate of Mercedes' passion.
> It seems that, rather foolishly Mercedes letters to Marlene detail very frequently her still ongoing love for Garbo. A suggestion that Marlene's estrangement from her director and lover Josef von Sternberg could be as a result of Mercedes' presence in Marlene's life. Maria calls her - as did Talullah Bankhead - "Dracula." As reported in Old Dyke.

A draft of her memoirs "Here Lies the Heart" can be found at the Rosenbach Museum.

Mercedes cultivated her appearance, always wearing black and white, a swirling cloak, and pointed shoes with a gold buckle.
Her black hair was cut short and slicked back, topped by an old fashioned tricorne hat.
When she lost the sight of an eye, she affected a black eye patch.
Famous names listed in "Here Lies the Heart":
- Duse,
- Caruso,
- Picasso,
- Matisse,
- Toscannini,
- Bernhardt,
- Rodin,
- Novello,
- Pavlova,
- Diaghilev,
- Noel Coward,
- Novello,
- Beaton,
- Marie Laurencin,
- Malvina Hoffman,
- Isadora Duncan,
- Nazimova,
- Eva le Gallienne,
- Katharine Cornell,
- Constance Collier.

*** *** ***

Famous bisexual and lesbians & members of the Sewing Circle

Laurette Taylor

Louise Brooks

Peggy Fears

Agnes Moorhead
A superb artist, no question about it!

Janet Gaynor

Gertrude Stein

Joan Crawford, a bisexual and insatiable nymphomaniac.

Author Lawrence Quirk said Joan slept with several fellow chorus girls while in New York City, and relates that Joan's press agent Jerry Asher told him Joan had a crush on early co-star Anita Page, and actually slept with Dorothy Sebastian, Gwen Lee, May Clark, and Stanwyck.

Dorothy Sebastian
Lover of Joan Crawford

Dorothy Sebastian.

She told Tallulah Bankhead that she loved to make love to Joan Crawford because she smelled so good. Apparently Crawford used different fragrance for each intimate or sensual part of her body.

(Stanwyck's press agent Helen Ferguson is quoted as saying "There is no doubt in my mind that Joan and Barbara were intimate on more than one occasion.")

Asher also said Joan Crawford was interested in Bette Davis in the 1930s (though not at the time *Baby Jane* was filming, which Davis claimed), when Davis had eyes for Joan's husband Franchot Tone.
Said Joan: "Franchot isn't interested in Bette, but I wouldn't mind giving her a poke if I was in the right mood. Wouldn't that be funny?"

Quirk also says that in her autobiography, Martha Raye claims she slept with Joan when they were both involved with the USO during WWII. Author Shaun Considine quotes director Vincent Sherman (himself a Joan-paramour) as saying, "When we were at Columbia (early '50s), there was a girl who was always hanging around (Joan). We often wondered about her."
Considine also quotes actress Louise Brooks that Joan was "one of those girls who went back and forth."
And quotes photographer Cecil Beaton, Joan's frequent crushes: "At one time she was insatiably interested in Dietrich...Then she moved on to Lillian Tashman, followed by the chief of her idols-- Greta Garbo."
Author Jane Ellen Wayne relates that when, on the set of '32's *Grand Hotel*, Greta Garbo took Joan's face in her hands after a chance meeting on-set, Joan was thrilled and later said, "If there was ever a time in my life when I might have become a lesbian, that was it." (Joan mentions the rather sexual excitement of this meeting in her April '73 Town Hall appearance.)

***   ***   ***

Dorothy Sebastian with her lover, Joan Crawford.

Two notorious lesbians, Gwen Lee and Dorothy Sebastian. Both had steamy sexual relation with Joan Crawford.

Marilyn Monroe: "Oh yes, Crawford. We went to her house from a cocktail party, feeling no pain. We went to the bedroom and went down on each other."

Photo: Pre-Code, Joan Crawford. She was an earthy and a passionate bisexual and a nymphomaniac who went though men, and women with the same ruthlessness she used to reach the top. Many photos of her with unidentified young women circulated in the pornographic underground of the era.

Author Fred Guiles says that Marilyn Monroe told her press agent that Joan had made a drunken pass at her one afternoon while Monroe was trying on clothes at Joan's house.

Crawford had a gigantic orgasm and shrieked like a maniac.

In tapes made for her psychiatrist shortly before her death, published in 2003 in a book by Matthew Smith, Marilyn said of Joan: "Oh yes, Crawford. We went to her house from a cocktail party, feeling no pain. We went to the bedroom and went down on each other.
Crawford had a gigantic orgasm and shrieked like a maniac.
Next time I saw her she wanted another round. I told her straight out I didn't enjoy it much, doing it with a woman. After I turned her down she became spiteful."
As reported by Helen Ferguson, Martha Raye, Vincent Sherman, Jane Ellen Wayne, Fred Guiles, Marilyn Monroe, and Matthew Smith.

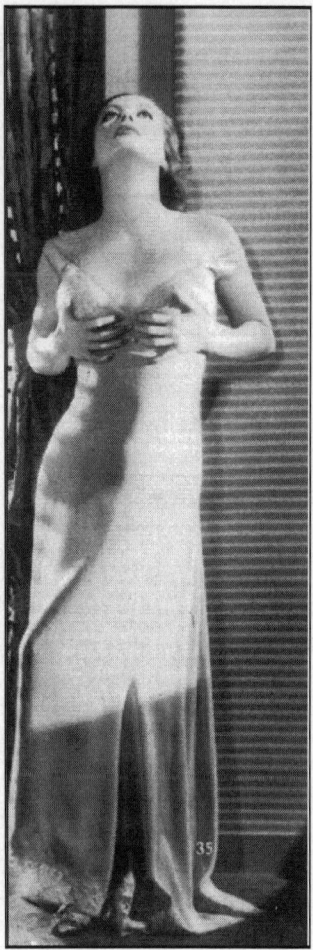

Photos, left, John Crawford with her sexual partner, Barbara Stanwyck. Right, Joan Crawford with her lover, Marilyn Dietrich.

Clara Bow on Joan Crawford and the running around town.

In a November 16, 1933 interview for the Kansas City Star, Clara Bow told John C. Moffitt: "It's funny. I really learned a lot during those dizzy years when Joan Crawford and I were running around town as the two hey-hey girls of Hollywood. Nobody thought I was learning anything. It seems rather funny to think that I was a sort of trademark for the flapper. The 'flapper' as a type seems about as antiquated as the suffragette or the vestal virgin, but I can remember when the whole country was standing on its ear over flappers.

They yelled about us in the pulpits and long-haired guys denounced us in the press. They made a world menace of us and all we were was a bunch of dizzy little gals with our skirts up to our knees and with Fiji Island haircuts. It seems sort of funny that anyone should have taken us seriously. But, boy, you should have seen some of the 'sinner beware!' letters I got."

Clara Bow, The "It Girl".

Clara Bow, raped by her father.
Bow was the incredible "it" girl of the silent screen era. This image was enhanced by various off-screen love affairs publicized by the tabloid press.

However, some Hollywood insiders considered her socially undesirable, especially in light of rumored sexual escapades with many famous men of the time. Bela Lugosi, Gary Cooper, Gilbert Roland, John Wayne, director Victor Fleming, and John Gilbert were reputed to be among her many lovers.

Bow was born in a tenement in Brooklyn, NY, the only surviving child of a dysfunctional family afflicted with mental illness and Dickensian poverty and physical and emotional abuse.
Her mother, Sarah Gordon, a sometime prostitute who was mentally ill as well as an epileptic, was noted for her public and frequent affairs with local firemen.
Her father, Robert Bow, was rarely present and whenever he was home, he was verbally and physically abusive to both wife and daughter.

Bow's father reportedly raped Clara when she was between the ages of 15 and 16 years old. Bow's alleged alcoholism, drug abuse, and mental instability were also becoming problems for the studios.
Budd Schulberg, the producer's son, said, "There was one subject on which the staid old Hollywood establishment would agree: Clara Bow, no matter how great her popularity, was a low life and a disgrace to the community" (The Schulberg quote appears in his memoir, Moving Pictures).
Not all of the negative rumors were true, but Bow probably did inherit mental instability from her mother. (Sources: Clara Bow org, We wear Lavender Bracelets)

*** *** ***

Lizabeth Scott. A magnificent actress.

In 1955, Scott, who never married, sued Confidential over allegations concerning her sexual preferences. In 1957 her film career came to an end with her role in Loving You (dir: Hal Kanter), Elvis Presley's second movie (although she appeared in an offbeat British film Pulp in 1972).

Since 1957 she has been seldom seen except for a few rare television appearances. Her downfall said insiders was caused by her sexual orientation. According to Diana McClellan's book on Sappho Hollywood, "The Girls," Scott was shunned late in the studio era for her sexual orientation. It was seen as an obscenity for Scott to be associated with lesbians as well as lesbian night clubs.

***   ***   ***

Some of the Hollywood divas found strength in clandestine feminine romantic and sexual friendship.

> Writer extraordinaire Axel Madsen in his fabulous book "The Sewing Circle" stated that some of the Hollywood divas, stars and starlets had enough of men, artifice, and glamour, they found solace, strength and understanding in clandestine feminine romantic and sexual friendship.
>
> Onscreen these women were the incarnations of turbid fantasies. Off-screen they depended on women who loved women, like that of poet-playwright Mercedes de Acosta, whose bed they shared in succession. Not only did lesbians live hidden lives, the public at large averted its eyes.
>
> Nobody wanted to know.
> Greta Garbo, Marlene Dietrich, Katharine Hepburn, and Barbara Stanwyck cultivated the movies' rich territory of sexual ambiguity as insolent, direct, kiss-me deadly females.

Katharine Hepburn
Brooks on Hepburn, "With men she acted like a man. With women, she acted like a woman, that's her style."

Alla Nazimova, queen of lesbianism glam of Hollywood.

Alla Nazimova

Oscar Wilde, one of the most famous homosexuals of the era.

Leslie Davies in her magnificent exposé on Hollywood's golden age of lesbian 'glam', wrote: "Homosexual men get all the credit for being fabulous, campy and gay, whereas the mythos of lesbians seems to involve a bad hair day and comfortable shoes. Evidently the stereotype is that gay men should decorate the house and make it pretty while gay women move the furniture."

*** *** ***

Bisexual Marie Prevost with stocking, one over the knee, the other rolled below the knee, and cuffed slouch boots, in 1918.

Bisexual Claudette Colbert

Claudette Colbert bathes in asses' milk in the 1932 film "The Sign of the Cross", directed by Cecil B. DeMille.

Colbert had steamy sexual relations with both women and men.
Crawford told Brooks who told Bankhead, "Colbert had the firmest nipples in Hollywood."
And Bankead replied furiously, "What's wrong with you girl, haven't you seen mine?"

Gloria Swanson loved the feminity in men and the masculinity in women.

Fifi D'Orsay. She was the most sophisticated one, next to Brooks.

Jean Acker.
"All the girls wanted to have her..." said Tallulah.

Ina Claire

Marlene Dietrich and Greta Garbo had a strange ongoing feud throughout their lives. Whereas both claimed to have never met one another, McLellan claims that the two appeared together in the silent film *The Joyless Street* in 1925 and had a brief affair that did not end well. Evidently Garbo held grudges long after she could remember what they were about. If legendary screen sirens Garbo and Dietrich were involved romantically with each other, they took the secret to their graves. In fact Garbo took all of her secrets to the grave. Soon after her career took off, Garbo became known as a recluse.

Throughout her lifetime she conducted no interviews, signed no autographs, attended no social functions and answered no fan mail. Today she is often associated with her famous line from *Grand Hotel*: "I want to be alone."

However, Garbo later commented, *"I never said, 'I want to be alone.' I only said, 'I want to be let alone.' There is all the difference."* (Sources: My opera.com, Answers.com, Speaking Colors Blogspot, Leslie Davis, The Examiner, Atlanta.)

Katharine Cornell.

Both Cornell and Azner were the lesbian partners of Nazimova, Greta Garbo and Marlene Dietrich.

Katharine Cornell in "The Age of Innocence" (1929).

Alla Nazimova

Nazimova with Rudolph Valentino in a scene from "Camille", 1921. Directed by Ray C. Smallwood.

Phyllis Haver with Ben Turpin posing for Mack Sennett, for his famous series "Bathing Beauties."

Greta Garbo lovers and sex partners (Men and women):
She was a notorious bisexual

Alla Nazimova	Einar Hanson
Aristoteles Onassis	Erich Maria Remarque
Barbara Barondess	Eva Le Gallienne
Barbara Stanwyck	Gary Cooper
Carl Brisson	Gaylor Hauser
Fifi D'Orsay	George Brent
Cecil Beaton	George Schlee
Cecile de Rothschild	George Tabori
Charles Addams	Gilbert Roland
Claire Koger	Irene Selznick
Clara Bow	John Barrymore
Claudette Colbert	John Gilbert
Count Bernadotte	Johnny Weissmüller
Count Wachtmeister	Leopold Stokowsky
Countess Bernadotte	Lili Damita
Countess Wachtmeister	Lilli Palmer
David Niven	Lilyan Tashman
Deborah Kerr	Louise Brooks
Edith Piaf	Marlene Dietrich

Mauritz Stiller	Rouben Mamoulian
Max Gumpel	Salka Viertel
Mercedes de Acosta	Sam Green
Mona Mårtenson	Sven Broman
Nils Asther	Sydney Guilaroff
Noël Coward	Tallulah Bankhead
Oona Munson	Valentina Schlee
Peter Viertel	Vera Schmiterlöw
Pola Negri	Wilhelm Sörenson
Prince Sigvard Bernadotte	Yul Bryner
Ramon Navarro	Zsa Zsa Gabor

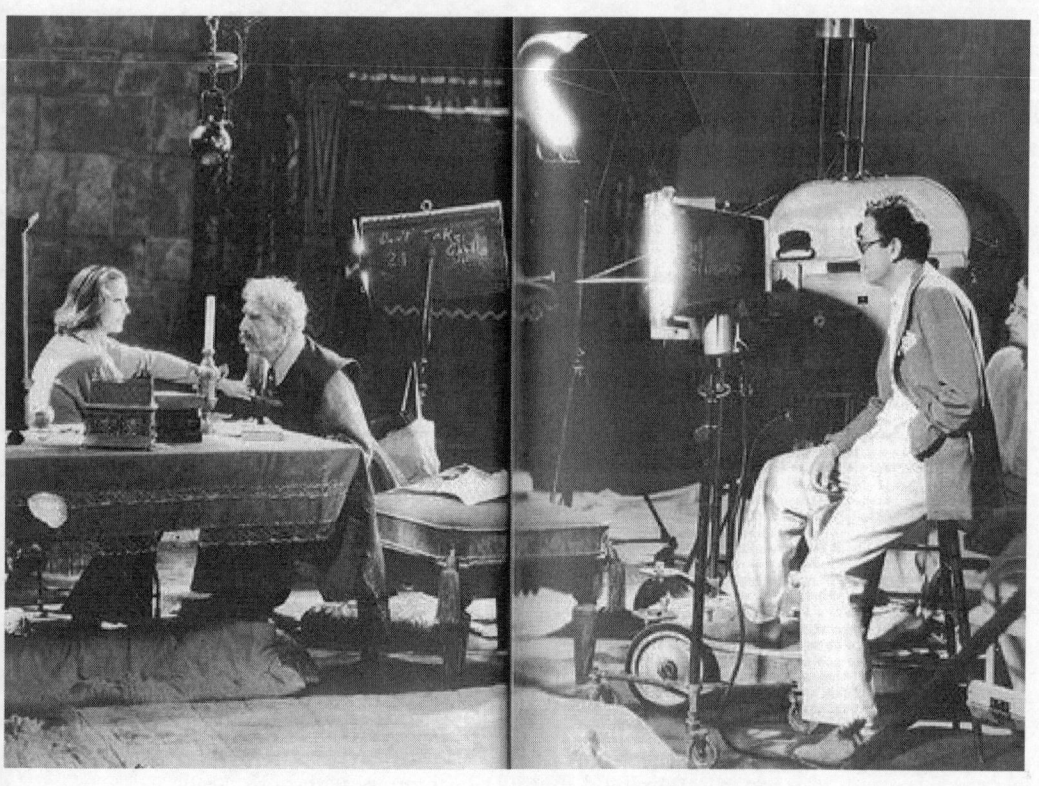

Greta Garbo in Queen Christina, 1933.

From left to right: Greta Garbo, C. Aubry Smith, Director Rouben Mamoulian and cinematographer Bill Daniels (far right). Mamoulian did Garbo constantly while directing her in "Queen Christina". He said Garbo loved to be kissed on the neck and her nipples.

What it was said about her affairs and lesbianism, and who said it:

- Louise brooks said that she has spent a night together, and that Greta Garbo was both charming and tender. She told film writer John Kobal, "She made a pass at me."
- Greta Garbo had a threesome with Marlene Dietrich, and Mercedes de Acosta.
- Director Mamoulian did Garbo constantly while directing her in "Queen Christina". He said Garbo loved to be kissed on the neck and her nipples.

- Garbo had a threesome with George Schlee and Aristoteles Onassis on this beast's yacht.
- Garbo had multiple threesomes with Oona Munson and Mercedes de Acosta. During the mid 1930s, Marlene Dietrich, and Tallulah Bankhead joined in, among others. De Acosta would later write to Dietrich to tell her how "wild and tender" Garbo was in bed.
- Lillian Tashman had multiple encounters with Garbo. A confident of Tashman claimed that both actresses enjoyed group sex with lesbians, and voyeurism.
- In her autobiography, Zsa Zsa Gabor stated "One Lifetime Is Not Enough" referring to that one night Greta Garbo seduced her.
- Irene Selznick, the daughter of Louis B. Mayer stated that Garbo tried to seduce her, and on two occasions she touched her breasts.
- In his biography, Sydney Guilaroff a well-known hairstylist in Hollywood claimed to have had long term sexual affairs and multiple encounters with both Greta Garbo and Ava Gardner.
- Erich Maria Remarque, the author of the 1929's "All Quiet on the Western Front," claimed that he had a "double affair" with Paulette Goddard and Greta Garbo.
- According to Fifi D'Orsay, she had a threesome with Greta Garbo and Bing Crosby.
- Barbara Barondess was Greta Garbo's stylist, and Marilyn Monroe's adopted big sister.
- She was also Garbo's co-star in the 1933 film "Queen Christina." When director Rouben Mamoulian offered her a role as a maid in Queen Christina (1933) she refused, because she thought the role he gave her was insignificant. However, when he told her she will be paid $9,000 for four days' work, she changed her mind and took the job. She and Garbo became lovers for a short time, but remained close friends for many years. She wrote about Garbo in her biography, "As an interior designer later on, I did her house. She used to come into my shop on Wilshire Boulevard and talk.

Photos: Above and below: Greta Garbo with Aristoteles Onassis. The Greek insatiable wild beast Aristoteles Onassis did Garbo non-stop, and Garbo had a threesome with George Schlee and Onassis on this beast's yacht.

George Schlee with Greta Garbo.

"George Schlee was Greta's companion and some kind of a manager. He was by her site from the 1940s to 1960s. It seems he wanted to marry Garbo. But he was married to Valentina Schlee. He couldn't get divorce. Again we are not sure that there was love between them. When Schlee died in 1964 Garbo was deeply shocked. She really cared for him and missed him until her final years.

They met through Valentina, Garbo's dress designer in New York in 1941. On the Riviera, in Cap d'Ail, George Schlee bought "Le Roc", a spacious and well protected house, which, naturally, has never been called anything besides Garbo's house."-Source: Garbo for Ever.

Greta Garbo and George Brent in "The Painted Veil". According to Lilli Palmer, Greta Garbo had an affair with her co-star George Brent while filming "The Painted Veil," Greta Garbo told Palmer that Brent was horny all the time but could not please her because he ejaculated too fast and went to sleep with two bottles of Bourbon.

- I think she was the dullest woman I ever met.
- I bought her first Renoirs. She begged me to take her to the auction sale where they were selling the paintings. She sat next to me and, when I bid over $300,000 for the two paintings, she almost had a heart attack... She was the tightest, most miserly figure who ever lived. She paid for the paintings that day, but never paid me my commission. I never asked for it. I knew she was a tightwad. She used people and rarely gave anything back." She told Marilyn Monroe, "She was stingy, but made up the difference in bed."
- In his biography, Johnny Weissmuller, the original Tarzan claimed that, in the 1930s, he had a steamy love affair with Garbo. During one of his regular fights with his wife Lupe Velez, he told Lupe that she should learn how to be lady in the living room and a whore in the bedroom, instead of being a "bitch all the time." The Mexican spitfire ferociously scratched his face, causing him serious injuries.
- According to Lilli Palmer, Greta Garbo had an affair with her co-star George Brent while filming "The Painted Veil," Greta Garbo told Palmer that Brent was horny all the time but could not please her because he ejaculated too fast and went to sleep with two bottles of Bourbon.
- Nils Asther had a threesome with Greta Garbo, Joan Crawford and Pola Negri.
- Mexican actor, Ramon Novaro known as the "Latin Lover" had a brief affair with Garbo while filming together "Mata Hari".
- Commenting on her affair with him, she said verbatim, "He was a man from the neck up."
- Ironically, both Rudolph Valentino and Novaro were nicknamed "Latin Lover", while in real life, both were gay.

*** *** ***

Anna Sten, (name at birth: Anjuschka Stenski Sudakewitsch, born in Kiev, Ukraine.) Allegedly, she was one of Garbo's sexual partners. A quote from Anna Sten in Nana (1934), "It's men who make women whatever they are." Nana (aka *Lady of the Boulevards* in the UK.) Sam Goldwyn was determined to make the next Garbo or Dietrich. But Sten never reached stardom.

Anna Sten

Marlene Dietrich

Marlene Dietrich's lovers and sexual partners:
(Just to name a few):

- Adlai Stevenson
- Alberto Giacometti
- Alla Nazimova
- Anna May Wong
- Anthony Quinn
- Bebe Daniels
- Berthold Held
- Bob Ritchie
- Brian Aherne
- Burgess Meredith
- Burt Bacharach
- Burt Lancaster
- Cary Grant
- Cecil Beaton
- Cesar Romero
- Charles Boyer
- Claire Waldof
- Clara Bow
- Claudette Colbert
- Colette
- Constance Talmadge
- David Niven

- Denise Parker
- Dolores Del Rio
- Dorothy MacKaill
- Douglas Fairbanks
- Eddie Fisher
- Edith Piaf
- Edward R. Murrow
- Elizabeth Alten
- Erich Maria
- Ernest Hemingway
- Errol Flynn
- Ferenc Molnar
- Fifi D'Orsay
- Frank Sinatra
- Fritz Lang
- Gary Cooper
- George Raft
- George S. Patton
- Gerard Philipe
- Gilda Gray
- Ginette Spanier
- Gloria Swanson
- Greg Bautzer
- Greta Garbo
- Hans Jaray
- Howard Hughes
- Humphrey Bogart
- Igo Sym
- Imperio Argentina
- Ina Claire
- Isadora Duncan
- James Gavin
- Jane Rogers
- Janet Gaynor
- Jean Acker
- Jean Arthur
- Jean Gabin
- Jimmy Stewart
- Joan Crawford
- Joe DiMaggio
- John F. Kennedy
- John Gilbert
- John O'Hara
- John Wayne
- Jorge Guinle
- Jose Iturbi
- Josef von Sternberg
- Joseph Kennedy
- Judy Garland
- Katharine Cornell
- Kirk Douglas
- Leo Lerman
- Leslie Howard
- Leyland Hayward
- Lili Damita
- Louise Brooks
- Marion Carstairs
- Marlon Brando
- Maurice Chevalier
- Mercedes de Acosta
- Michael Todd
- Michael Wimding
- Milton Berle
- Montgomery Clift
- Ona Munson
- Orson Welles
- Otto Preminger
- Peggy Fears
- Pola Negri
- Reginald Gardiner
- Richard Barthelmess
- Richard Talbert
- Robert F. Kennedy
- Ronald Colman
- Rudolph Seibert
- Tallulah Bankhead
- Tyrone Power
- Victor McLaglen

- Willi Forst
- William Saroyan
- Yul Bryner

FBI Files on Marlene Dietrich.
Copies from the files on the following pages.

The FBI had a file of 230 pages on Marlene Dietrich at the FBI Headquarters in Washington, D.C.
The file contains approximately 200 discernable pages. The files date from 1935 to 1948. Subject matters include:
Documentation of an FBI investigation started in 1942, because of a rumor that Dietrich was apart of a German collaboration movement in United States and France. Dietrich's tax problems.
Information from Dietrich's intercepted mail and telegram correspondences. The amount of scrutiny Marlene Dietrich was under is demonstrated by a memo containing information from a employee of the famous Schwab's Drug Store on Sunset Boulevard in Los Angeles, who would attempt to eavesdrop on Dietrich's conversations when she was in the store.
Information from an informant about an affair with John Wayne. Dietrich's relationship with Jean Gabin, a war hero and the most popular French actor of the prewar era.
Gabin's affair with Ginger Rogers. Dietrich's relationship with her husband Rudolf Sieber and her attempts to aid his gaining of United Sates citizenship.
Marlene Dietrich died in Paris, of kidney failure, at the age of 90.

*** *** ***

Marlene Dietrich

SAC Los Angeles - 2 -

Mrs. Willebrandt stated ▓▓▓ and Miss Dietrich are intensely close and their aim in this country is to get anyone who could be a popular star on the Continent to return and make pictures for Continental Films. They are trying to get Jean Gabin, ▓▓▓ (phonetic) and Rence Claire (phonetic) to return and make such pictures. Mrs. Willebrandt feels that Miss Dietrich is doing work for this company.

It was the opinion of Mrs. Willebrandt that Miss Dietrich is directly connected with these collaborationists, that she is an active agent and that there is some means of direct communication between them. She mentioned that film people are either so uneducated or so vain that they are easy prey to such designs.

It is desired that an immediate discreet investigation be undertaken by your office concerning Miss Dietrich in order to ascertain whether she may be engaged in activities inimical to the national defense of the United States. The Bureau should be kept promptly and fully advised of all developments in this connection.

Mrs. Willebrandt has indicated that she will be in California for the next week after which she will return to Washington. It is desired that the Washington Field Office make arrangements to interview Mrs. Willebrandt further for any additional information she may have concerning this matter.

Very truly yours,

John Edgar Hoover
Director

cc Washington

Copy of a cover letter signed by Edgar Hoover from the FBI files on Marlene Dietrich.

Marlene Dietrich's gallery of some of her lovers and sexual partners (Men and women)

Jean Gabin, the love of her life.

The most famous lesbians were:

Agnes Moorehead,
Alla Nazimova,
Alice B. Toklas,
Alma Rubens,
Anna Sten. She was dubbed "Goldwyn's Folly."
Armen Ohanian,
Barbara Lamarr,
Barbara Stanwyck,
Beatrice Lillie,
Clara Bow,
Claudette Colbert,
Constance Collier,
Constance Trevor,
Christa Winsloe,
Dorothy Arzner,
Dorothy Gish,
Dorothy Knapp,
Dorothy MacKaill,
Dorothy Sebastian,
Elsie de Wolfe,
Elsie Ferguson,
Eva Le Gallienne,
Faith Bacon,
Fifi D'Orsay,
Gay Russell,
Genie Fursa,
Gertrude Stein,
Gilda Gray,
Gloria Swanson,
Greta Garbo,
Gwen Lee,
Harriet Hammond,
Helen Arlen,
Helen Menken,
Isadora Duncan (A famous dancer and choreographer),
Janet Gaynor,
Jean Acker,
Joan Crawford,
Juanita Hensen,
Judith Anderson,
Judy Garland,
June Brewster,
Katharine Cornell,
Katharine Hepburn,
Laurette Taylor,
Lilian Gish,
Lili Damita,
Lilli Palmer,
Lilyan Tashman,
Lizabeth Scott,
Louise Brooks,
Mae Marshall,
Marie Prevost,
Marilyn Monroe. (She had an affair with Barbara Stanwyck, Crawford, among others.)
Marilyn Vega
Marion O'Day,
Marla English,
Marlene Dietrich,
Martha Raye,
Mary Thurman,
May Clark,
Mercedes de Acosta who seems to have slept with everyone.
Myrna Darby,
Myrna Loy,
Natacha Rambova (she was actually Winifred Shaughnessy, and the wife of bisexual Rudolph Valentino).
Natalie Clifford Barney,
Nelda Kinkaid,
Oona Munson (Husbands: Director Ernst Lubitsch; Charlie Chaplin).

Patsy Kelly,
Peggy Fears,
Peggy Hopkins Joyce,
Pepi Lederer,
Phyllis Haver,
Pola Negri,

Sally Forest (Unsubstantiated rumors),
Sybil Thorndyke,
Sylvia Sidney,
Tallulah Bankhead,
Theda Bara,
Violet Arnol

Publicity still from The Masks of the Devil (1928), starring Alma Rubens and John Gilbert.

Dorothy Gish

Barbara Lamarr

Sylvia Sydney

Mae Marshall

Barbara Stanwyck

Theda Bera: The screen's first sex symbol.

Gilda Ray

Myrna Darby performed in the Ziegfeld Follies of 1927.

Marilyn Vega

Pola Negri.
At one time in Hollywood's history, Negri was larger than any screen.

Pola Negri

Pola Negri was a notorious bisexual, who had numerous affairs with Greta Garbo and Marlene Dietrich. She slept with both men and women. She was madly in love with bisexual cinema legend, Rudolph Valentino. Negri was the mysterious "Woman in black" who visited the tomb of Valentino on a daily basis, always hiding her face with a black veil. Every day, she would bring a dozen of white and red roses to her departed lover. She stood by his tomb, cried a lot, polished his name on the plaque of his tomb, and dissipated in the shadows of mystery and sorrow... later on, and for years (until 1961) many other women would do the same. One of them was Estrellita de Rejil; she appeared for the last time on August 23, 1989.

Photo, left: Pola Negri with Rudolph Valentino.
On the next page: Negri at Valentino's tomb.

Emil Jannings, Pola Negri in the 1919 film "Madame Dubarry", one of Germany's first successes on the foreign market.

Director: Ernst Lubitsch.
Screenplay: Norbert Falk, and Hans Kraly.
Directors Photography:
Fritz Arno Wagner and Theodor Sparkuhl.
Cast included:
Pola Negri,
Emil Jannings,
Reinhold Schunzel,
Harry Liedtke.

Mary Brian

Josephine Baker

Hope Williams

Lilyan Tashman slept with everybody.

Despite her elegant and fragile façade, she was ferocious in bed, according to Pola Negri, who also said the same thing about Tallulah Bankead.
When asked, if it was true, Tallulah replied:
"My daddy warned me about men and booze but he didn't say a word about women and cocaine!"
It was Lilyan Tashman, an openly bisexual glamour girl, who taught Greta Garbo how to move, talk, and look like a movie star. Lilyan Tashman became one of Garbo's first female lovers in Hollywood.
Joan Crawford said that, Lily (Lilyan Tashman) had several orgies with Greta Garbo, Claudette Colbert, Louise Brooks, Stanwyck, Tallulah Bankhead, and Mercedes de Acosta.
Yes, it gets so confusing!!

Lilyan Tashman

Tallulah Bankhead

Below, from L to R: Kurt Weill, Lotte Lenya, von Rechts, Eleonora Mendelssohn, and Francesco von Mendelssohn in 1935 in New York.

Lili Damita with pervert Eric von Stroheim, with whom she had a brief affair.
Damita slept with both men and women.

Hedy Lamarr

Hedy Lamarr loved both men and women. She was married six times and raped by men and women alike.
She ended up penniless, and refused any financial support from friends and peers. Frank Sinatra, Dean Martin, and Lucille Ball came to the rescue, but she refused their help.

Beatrice Lillie

Sally Forrest. Rumors were never substantiated.

From the landscape of stars' homosexuality in Hollywood

Are they gay? Homosexuals? Bisexuals?
How to find out?
Look in the "Doom Book."

The "Doom Book" was a list created by Hollywood studios' bosses listing included actresses, actors directors, and others "whose private lives were contrary to public morals.: consequently, they should not be employed by the Hollywood studios.

*** *** ***

Homosexuals, Gays, and Bisexuals Male Stars (The most recognizable):

- 1-Cary Grant
- 2-Robert Taylor
- 3-Dany Kaye. His favorite lover was Laurence Olivier.
- 4-Randolph Scott
- 5-Rock Hudson
- 6-James Dean
- 7-Montgomery Clift
- 8-Liberace
- 9-Toni Curtis
- 10-Jean Cocteau
- 11-Jean Marais
- 12-Elton John
- 13-Rudolph Valentino
- 14-Laurence Olivier
- 15-Tyrone Power
- 16-Charles Laughton
- 17-Peter O'Tool
- 18-Noel Coward
- 19-William Haines
- 20-Vincente Minnelli
- 21-Tony Perkins
- 22-Director George Cukor. (Had oral sex with Clark Gable)
- 23-Vincent Price
- 24-Van Johnson
- 25-Raymond Burr (His lover was actor Robert Benevides.)
- 26-William Desmond Taylor
- 27-Alan Ladd

Robert Taylor

Photo: Judy Holliday, Jose Ferrer, Gloria Swanson, and George Cukor at an Oscar party in 1951. Director George Cukor had oral sex with Clark Gable.

George Cukor's private life was well known in Hollywood. His Sunday afternoon pool parties were legendary in gay circles, having been described at lurid detail by some of the party guests, including writer John Rechy. His home, decorated by actor-turned interior designer William Haines, was the spot for Hollywood homosexuals to gather.

The close knit group included Haines and his partner Jimmie Shields, Alan Ladd, W. Somerset Maugham, James Vincent, screenwriter Rowland Leigh, costume designers Orry-Kelly, Robert Le Maire, actors John Darrow, Robert Walker, Anderson Lawler, Robert Seiter and Tom Douglas. Frank Horn secretary to Cary Grant, was a frequent guest.

Alan Ladd
Photo above: Alan Ladd and Veronica Lake in "This Gun for Hire", 1942.

Charles Laughton

Born: July 1, 1899 in Victoria Hotel, Scarborough, Yorkshire, England.

Died: December 15, 1962 in Hollywood, California. Popularity today: Highly revered and remembered by cinema buffs and experts, but almost forgotten by the general public. Film: The Private Life of Henry VIII.
His wife, actress Elsa Lanchester wrote in her biography that he was gay. They had stormy relationship.

Laurence Olivier

Born: May 22, 1907 in Surrey, UK. Died: July 11, 1989 in West Sussex, UK.
At one time in his life, his bisexuality became a heavy burden on his theatrical career, especially in the Shakespearian entourage in London. He had sexual relationship with Noel Coward, and Charles Laughton.

William Desmond Taylor

At the beginning, many believed that Taylor was a real stud.

In fact, he was a pussycat, a sissy, a homosexual with passion for young boys.

During the investigation of his murder, the police discovered in his hidden lingeries and silk-lavender underwear closet, all sorts, shapes and sizes of fetishes, nightgowns, and photographs of young boys, who were procured for him by his valet Henry Peavy, an expert in "down-rub."

This shady character was arrested by the police while soliciting the boys.

The boys were brought to a room located near the house of Taylor, and rented for the master by Peavy. The room was full of pornographic photos, and the upper parts of some walls were decorated with obscene sexual acts.

Some of the photos were published in the newspapers with disturbing commentaries.

The police also discovered evidence linking him to narcotics trafficking and bootlegging. The Oscar winning director George Hopkins who knew Taylor very well confirmed William Desmond Taylor's homosexuality and sexual acts with young boys.

***   ***   ***

Rock Hudson's lovers (Men and women):

- Tom Clark
- Jill St. John
- Jack Coates
- March Christian
- Liberace
- Armistead Maupin
- Joan Crawford
- Yvonne De Carlo
- George Nader
- Edie Adams
- Elaine Stritch
- Errol Flynn
- Jim Nabors
- Marylin Maxwell
- Piper Laurie
- Tyrone Power
- Armistead Maupin

James Dean
A well-known homosexual in the close circle of Hollywood.

James Dean and his lover Sal Mineo.

Out of the closet entertainers:

Alan Cumming
Alexis Arquette
Amelie Mauresmo
Andy Bell
Anthony Perkins
Barry Mannilow
Boy George
Chastity Bono
David Geffen
David Hyde Pierce
Dirk Bogarde
Ellen Degenares
Ian McKellen
Jodie Foster
John Barrowman
Johnny Mathis
Lance Bass

Little Richard
Morrissey
Nigel Hawthorne
Portia de Rossi
Raymond Burr
Robert Gant
Sam Fox
Sandra Bernhard
Simon Callow
Sinead O'Connor
Sir John Gielgud
Stephen Fry
Stephen Gately
Tommy Kirk
Tony Curtis
Tracy Chapman

Young Clarke Gable engaged in oral sex with fellow MGM player William Haines.

John Wayne's use of casting sessions to seduce young male contract players.

> As revealed in Brownwing's book, it was not just aspiring actresses who were subjected to humiliating ordeals in order to secure advancement.
>
> "Whilst it is quite well-known that the young Clarke Gable engaged in oral sex with fellow MGM player William Haines in order to establish himself at the studio, less well known are legendary hard man John Wayne's use of casting sessions to seduce young male contract players," claims Brownwing. "
>
> During the 1940s the outwardly conservative and heterosexual Wayne would regularly attend screen tests with director John Ford, in order to size up potential conquests.

He'd get Ford to order the young hopefuls to take off their shirts and enact scenes which required them to lift heavy objects or bend over a lot."

When he'd picked out his likely targets, Wayne would arrange for Ford to call them back to the studio - usually late at night - for a bogus final screen test.

Instead of the director and a camera crew, the bewildered young actors would find themselves alone in an otherwise deserted studio with an amourous Wayne, who would typically be clad only in a Stetson and a pair of pearl handled Colt .45s holstered on his gunbelt.

MGM player William Haines (top) and Clarke Gable (below) were engaged in oral sex.

John Wayne

John Wayne's seduction technique

This seduction technique proved surprisingly successful for 'The Duke' - his conquests allegedly included:
- **Randolph Scott,**
- **Joel McCrea,**
- **Montgomery Clift**, with whom he had a torrid affair during the making of Red River in 1948.

Two other male stars to suffer unwanted attention were Rock Hudson and James Dean.
"Elizabeth Taylor reportedly came on to them very strongly during the making of "Giant," so they put out the rumour that they were both gay," says Brownwing.
"This proved so successful that Hudson kept up the gay pretence for years in order to ward off the attentions of notorious female sexual predators like Doris Day.
He even hired male models to pose as his boyfriends."
So few people were aware of the truth that even a hooker who had slept with Rock tried to sell a story to the press claiming that she was so hot she'd turned Rock Hudson straight! Luckily, nobody believed her.

Randolph Scott with his lover Cary Grant.

Randolph Scott (seduced by John Wayne) had a short affair with Cary Grant. And Scott also had an affair with Eroll Flynn. In fact, they have lived together for 6 months.

Cary Grant and Randolph Scott; two lovers in a "cachette".
In fact, they have lived together for 6 months.

Joel McCrea, seduced by John Wayne.

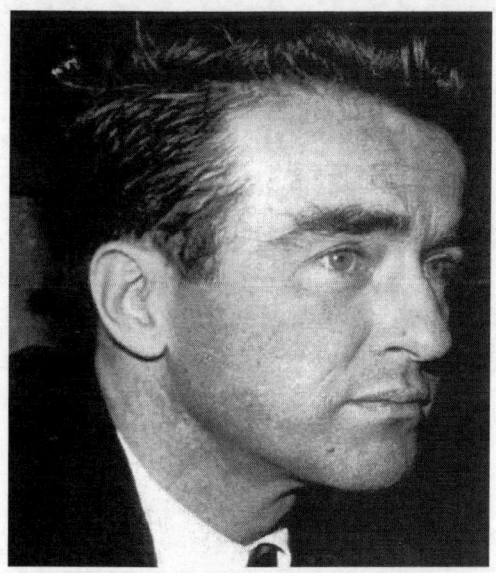

Montgomery Clift; he had a torrid affair with John Wayne during the making of "Red River" in 1948.

Phony Hollywood and fake "Latin Lovers": All were homosexuals and bisexuals, except one!

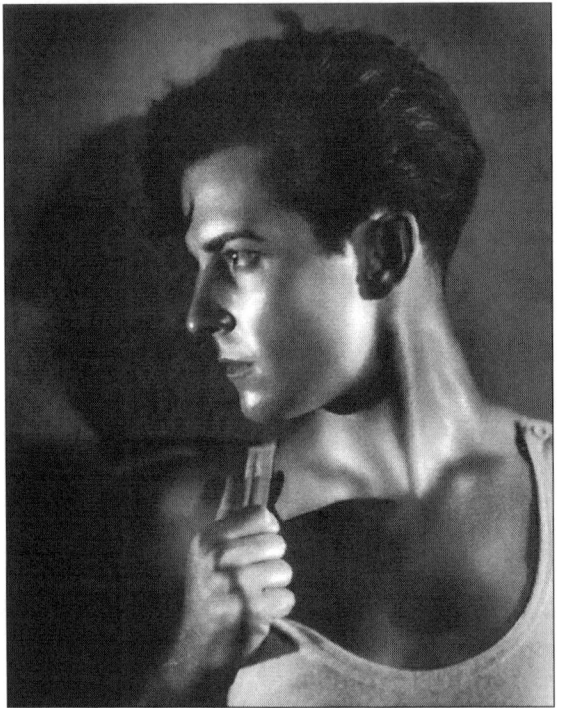

Ramon Novarro

Gilbert Roland

Antonio Moreno

Bisexual actor Ramon Novarro and Norma Shearer in "The student Prince in old Heidelberg", 1927, directed by Ernst Lubitsch.

What a vicious circle of perverts, sluts and cheaters

And while Irving Thalberg was fooling around, his wife Norma Shearer began numerous affairs with straight and gay actors like Ramon Novarro. And while Novarro was doing his things with Shearer, Gilbert Roland (Born Luis Antonio Damaso de Alonso in Chihuahua, Mexico) was doing him.
And while (and after) Roland was doing Novarro, Constance Bennett, Norma Talmadge, and Clara Bow were doing Roland according to Ava Gardner. At the age of 19, Gilbert Roland had his first break, when his lover Clara Bow gave him a role in her 1925 film *The Plastic Age*; this was Roland's first time screen credit.

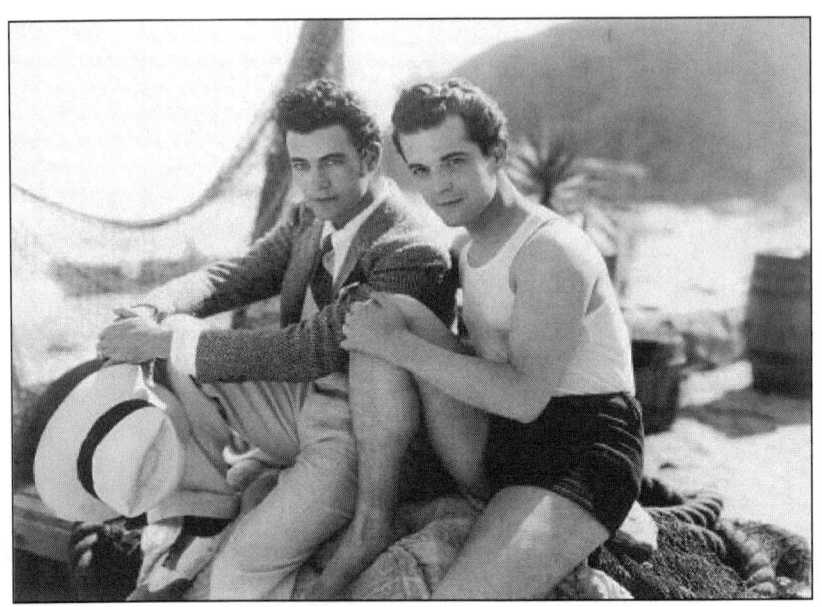

Ramon Novarro with his lover Gilbert Roland (left) 1930.

Harry Cohn: "Who do you think your wife is fucking tonight?"

Hollywood was a mobile bordello. According to Bette Davis, everybody was fucking everybody. And hustler Harry Cohn was the best to summarize the situation; over a dinner, that gathered some Columbia directors and big stars, Cohn asked one of his new Jewish writers, "Who do you think your wife is fucking tonight?"
According to authors Robin Cross and John Marriott, at press conferences to announce a new film, Cohn constantly referred to the male and female leads as "The prick and the cunt."
Plenty of written evidence quotes Cohn as remarking, "This time the prick will be played by...and the cunt by..."

Harry Cohn with Judy Holliday during a dinner at the Cocoanut Drove.

Hollywood is fake, and 80% of its major stars are equally phony!

To give you an idea how phony was Hollywood: The studios presented Rudolph Valentino (Italian) and Ramon Novarro (Mexican) as the essence of masculinity, the savvy, dashing passionate and exotic macho-men, and nicknamed them "The Latin Lover", while in real life, both Valentino and Novarro were notorious bisexuals.

In fact, Valentino before he became a cinema legend, was a male prostitute, a "lounge lizard", a professional gigolo, and a dancer for hire in Manhattan, New York.

He was arrested twice, and charged for male prostitution. He was caught in the act at Mrs. Georgia Thym brothel.

The tabloids called him the Italian Tango dancer who "wore corsets and a wristwatch", two items considered un-manly at the time. Two hookers and an Italian friend bailed him out! Worth mentioning here, that when Valentino became a famous star, Hollywood's studios made his criminal record and dossier disappear from the New York City police files.

All the women he lived with and/or married (Acknowledged four; all left him without regret) were notorious lesbians and bisexuals like him, to name a few: Jane Acker who slept with Alla Nazimova who slept with Natasha Rambova who slept with Gloria Swanson who slept with Pola Negri who slept with Joan Crawford who slept with Marilyn Monroe. All his marriages were "Lavender marriages." But Hollywood's deceit did not stop with Valentino and Novarro. In his early films, Antonio Moreno (A Spanish-born actor/director import) often played the Latin Lover too; in real life, he was bisexual.

In the 1920s and early 1030s, the vogue for the exotic Latins (as opposed to Latinos) like Valentino, Novarro, Moreno et al proved so popular among female cinemagoers, that actors actually concocted phony identities to pass, such as Jewish actor Jacob Krantz who was reborn "Ricardo Cortez." When people found out he wasn't actually Spanish, he tried to claim that he was at least French, which also proved untrue, according to Amoeba.

Tom Mix: A Hollywood's phony hero, a horse thief, and a deserter.

Photo: Tom Mix

Is Governor Arnold the most highly paid actor in the history of American motion pictures as he has claimed? No! The most highly paid actor in the history of American motion pictures is the western/cowboy superstar Tom Mix. In 1920, he used to earn as high as $20,000 a week plus a big cut. He was the "model for the dandyish, squeaky-clean movie cowboy that was much parodied in later years." Signing on with the Fox Film Corporation in 1917, the studio found for him the role that would catapult him to stardom: The Untamed.

In other words, Mix was a role model.
Really?
On screen or in real life?
Well, Mix was neither a role model, nor a hero, or the clean cut All-American specimen.
The studio marketed him as a great horseman, a valiant soldier, a bona-fide hero. In reality, Mix was a deserter, not an exceptional horseman, but a horse thief.
The studio presented him as a former Marshall, a Texas Ranger, a hero in the Spanish American War, an intrepid who charged up San Juan Hill with Roosevelt's Rough Riders and a rider with Pancho Villa. All these claims were false. They are the fabrication of Hollywood.
In fact, Mix deserted his military post at Fort Hancock, New Jersey, he was court martialed, and sent to prison when they caught him stealing horses.
He was as phony as Rudolph Valentino.

*** *** ***

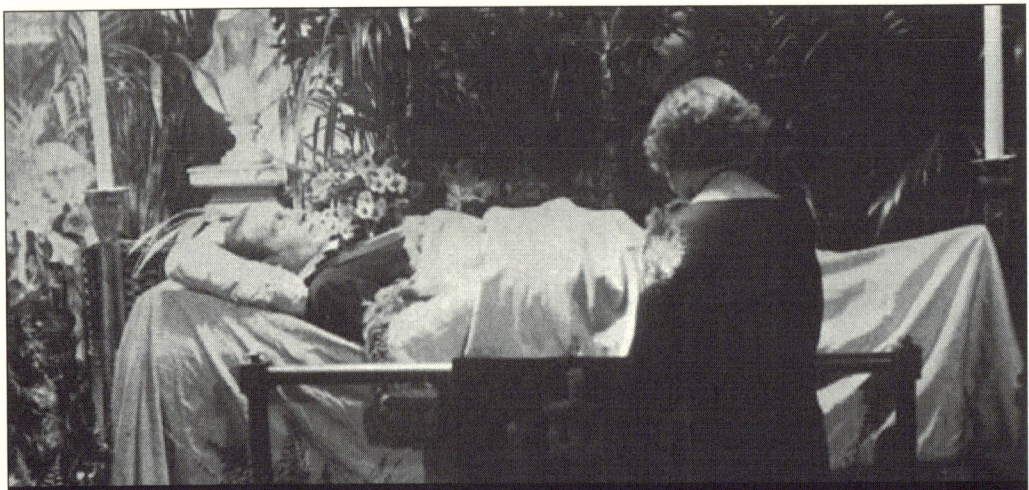

Pola Negri and Rudolph Valentino last moment.

Rudolph Valentino:

Rudolph Valentino (1895-1926) became a legend of the silver screen, and an icon of the silent screen.
While living in New York, Valentino was arrested for male prostitution. He is remembered for starring in The Sheik (1921).

*** *** ***

Rudolph Valentino and wife for a few months, Natacha Rambova.

Rudolph Valentino:

He landed in New York where he worked for a while as a dancer and obtained a certain local fame. It has been said that during this period he also was a gigolo and that he had judicial troubles for prostitution-related matters.
He next joined an operetta company that soon disbanded in Utah; from there he reached San Francisco, California, where he met the actor Norman Kerry, who convinced him to try a career in cinema, still in the silent era.
After a dozen films, that made him quite famous, in 1919 he was married for a few hours to Jean Acker (1893-1978), a part-Cherokee film starlet who was a lesbian; the marriage was reportedly never consummated and they were divorced in 1923. He then achieved full success in films in 1921 with "The Four Horsemen of the Apocalypse".

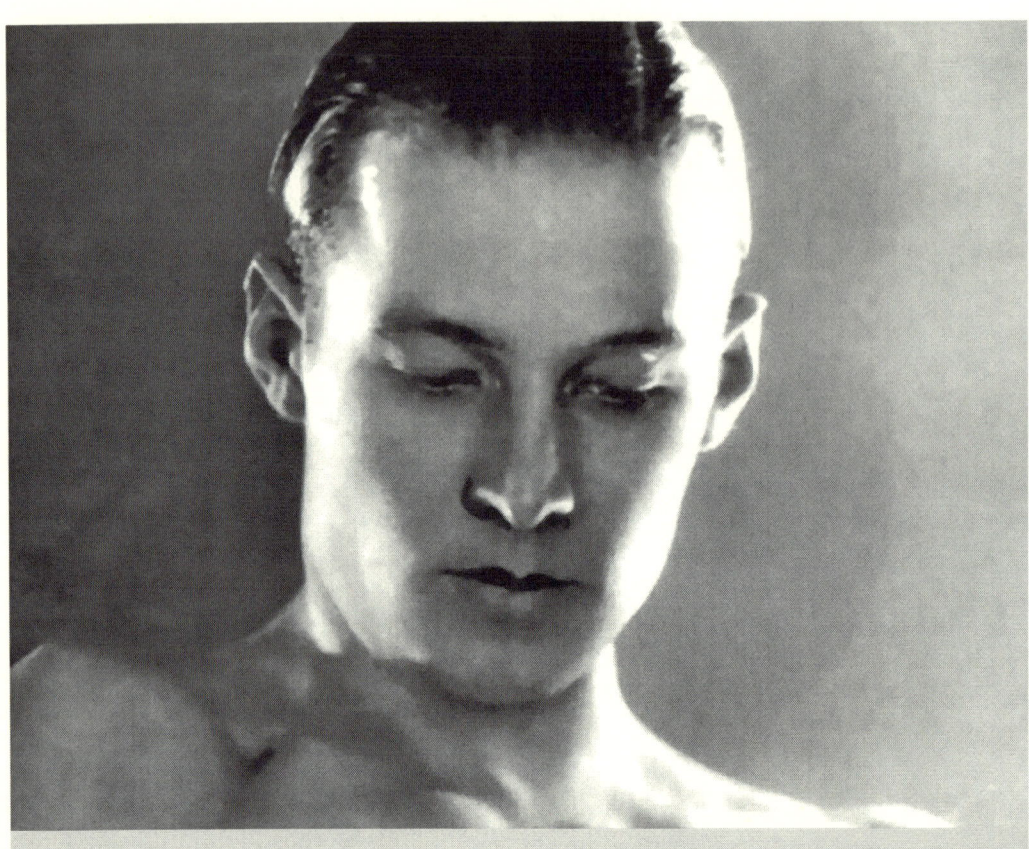

Rudolph Valentino

On May 13, 1922, in Mexicali, Mexico, Valentino married actress Natacha Rambova. This resulted in him being jailed for bigamy, since his divorce from Acker was not yet final. They remarried a year later.

Rudolph Valentino romances Alice Terry in "The Four Horsemen of the Apocalypse."

Latin Lover, Ricardo Montalban, a real man!

One of the very few Latin Lovers who did not belong to this scandalous milieu was Ricardo Montalban, a perfect gentleman with impeccable reputation, and high moral standards.
In 1944, Ricardo Montalban married Georgiana Young, the half-sister of the film actress Loretta Young.
The couple went on to raise four children in Los Angeles: Mark, Victor, Laura and Anita. Georgiana Young died in 2007.
Montalban became Hollywood's original "Latin Lover" in 1947.

Ricardo Montalbán and Esther Williams in the film "On an Island With You" (1948).

Hollywood's Nymphomaniacs and Piece of Meat!
What it was said by Hollywood's insiders

"Remember this, never forget it, you're just a piece of meat."- 1950's studio boss Harry Cohn, talking to actress Kim Novak.

Kim Novak   Harry Cohn

Capucine: "They fucked each other so much...women began to smell semen, and men perfume."
Louis B. Mayer: "A woman's ass is for her husband, not theatergoers."
Clark Gable: "Give those babes (Hollywood's actresses) the freedom and equality they are screaming for...and the first thing they will do...spread their legs."

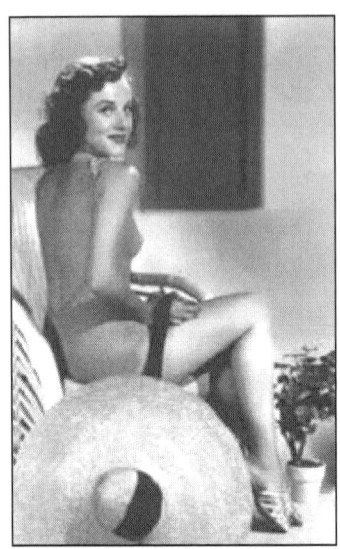

Paulette Goddard in a sexually provocative pose.
Why?
Because, this is what Hollywood's stars do! Show their front and their derriere. Talent is not always a prerequisite.

Anita Loos: "To place in the limelight a great number of people (actresses and actors) who ordinarily would be chambermaids and chauffeurs, and give them unlimited power and wealth, is bound to produce disastrous results."
(A. Loos, April 26, 1888 – August 18, 1981. She was an American screenwriter, playwright and author.)
Jean Gabin: "98% of the divas of Hollywood were "baptized" in the casting couch."
Harry Cohn: "Who do you think your wife is fucking tonight?"

According to authors Robin Cross and John Marriott, at press conferences to announce a new film, Cohn constantly referred to the male and female leads as "The prick and the cunt."
Plenty of written evidence quotes Cohn as remarking, "This time the prick will be played by...and the cunt by..."

Louis B. Mayer once said to a star "Just sit there, look beautiful, and the camera will take of the rest."

Vivien Leigh: "I am an actress, a great actress. Great actresses have lovers, why not?
I have a husband and I have lovers. Like Sarah Bernhardt."

Hollywood's Nymphomaniacs and Insatiable Stars

Women: The most notorious ones were:

- 1- Grace Kelly did more than 35 stars, 6 directors, had affairs with 46 men, including one night stand, and several young European men during her marriage.
- 2- Joan Crawford, who loved rough sex.
- 3- Clara Bow, twice as much as Joan Crawford.
- 4- Talullah Bankhead
- 5- Mae West
- 6- Jean Harlow
- 7- Lupe Velez, who once said in her juicy Mexican accent: "He (Gary Cooper) has the biggest dick in town...."
- 8- Mary Astor
- 9- Alice White
- 10- Dolores Del Rio

Clara Bow.
Photo: Clara Bow, drama queen and notorious nymphomaniac of Hollywood.

To the insiders, Clara Bow was known as Hollywood's "insatiable nymphomaniac." Her sexual appetite was legendary.

Clara Bow, the "It Girl."
The three most notorious nymphomaniacs in Hollywood were Grace Kelly, Clara Bow, and Joan Crawford

---

A Hollywood technician who worked on the set of one of her film said: "She could service the whole crew in one single night..." By "service" he meant "to have sex with." One night, the "It Girl," Clara Bow, took on the entire University of Southern California "Thundering Herd" football team during a "gangbanging" weekend party. On that night, she slept with 19 men. Bow's other conquests included Eddie Cantor, Gary Cooper and Bela Lugosi. On Cooper, she said: "He was hung like a horse and could go all night long, the best."

Some of Clara Bow's lovers:

258

Grace Kelly; an enormous sex drive.

Grace Kelly; a nymphomaniac with an insatiable sex appetite.

Gore Vidal on Grace Kelly: "Grace almost always laid the leading man. She was famous for that in this town." According to biographer Wendy Leigh, at age 22 Kelly had an off-set romance with both Gary Cooper and director Fred Zinnemann. Grace fell hard for Coop on the film.
Although Cooper was married, he was separated from his wife Rocky and in the middle of a tempestuous relationship with actress Patricia Neal. Coop was the start of a string of romances with much older men.
In Grace's case, her passionate sexual nature went against the Fifties notion that good girls didn't until they got married.

Grace Kelly with Oleg Cassini in 1954.

Grace, however, did and often.

She was addicted to sex in all its forms and "positions."

People Magazine wrote: "It was this contrast that fascinated filmmakers including Hitchcock. By this time Kelly was clearly far from innocent.

In late 1948, she fell in love with Don Richardson, one of her teachers at the Academy. The liaison lasted two years in the face of tremendous pressure from her family to end it. When she took him home to meet her parents, her mother went through Richardson's personal effects and found not only his divorce papers but also a packet of condoms.

In spite of parental disapproval, Kelly continued to see Richardson, along with a host of others including the Shah of Iran. While working, Grace met actor Gene Lyons.

Grace Kelly and Clark Gable in a scene from "Mogambo".

Grace Kelly and Ray Milland; add him to the list of her lovers.

Like Richardson, Gene was married, although he was in the process of getting an annulment.
While shooting Mogambo in 1953, a drama set in the Kenyan jungle which centers on the love triangle portrayed by Kelly, Clark Gable and Ava Gardner, she had an affair with Gable and commented: "What else is there to do if you're alone in a tent in Africa with Clark Gable?"
The next relationship almost ruined her career.
She met Ray Milland while working on Dial M For Murder. Milland fell head over heels in love with Kelly. When Milland's wife Muriel found out, she threw him out of the house. Kelly found herself written up in the tabloids as a home wrecker.
Gossip columnist Hedda Hopper spread rumors that the actress was a nymphomaniac.
The relationship finally ended when Milland realized how much it would cost him in a divorce. Kelly herself was always discreet, remarking simply in her defense: "As an unmarried woman, I was thought to be a danger."
It appears that Kelly didn't learn her lesson from the relationship with Milland. She next embarked on a torrid affair with William Holden who played her husband in The Bridges At Tokyo-Ri. Holden was willing to divorce his wife Brenda Marshall but the - relationship ended when Holden admitted he'd had a vasectomy.
Kelly's next conquest was Bing Crosby, her co-star in The Country Wife, who was recently widowed.
Ironically Bing Crosby hadn't wanted Kelly for the role of his wife Georgie Elgin, considering her too beautiful. Kelly proved her worth by winning a Best Actress Oscar for the role, just beating Judy Garland.
Her next relationship did little to reassure her parents. Designer Oleg Cassini had been smitten with Kelly ever since he had seen Mogambo.
After being introduced in a New York restaurant, Cassini pursued Kelly relentlessly. When she flew to the South of France for To Catch A Thief, she sent Cassini a postcard inviting him to follow her.
While Grace Kelly wanted to marry Cassini, she still craved her parents' approval.
Her mother was the first to meet Cassini and was not impressed. Although the designer came from an aristocratic Russian family and had grown up in Florence, he was also twice divorced with two children.

Years later, it was rumored that she was pregnant with Cassini's child and had an abortion. Cassini was not the only man she was seeing; she also spent time with French actor Jean-Pierre Aumont. When pictures of the two appeared in the tabloids, Kelly suspected that Aumont had tipped off photographers.

On a visit to the Cannes Film Festival in 1955, Kelly was persuaded to visit Monaco by Olivia de Havilland's husband Pierre Galante. An audience was arranged with Prince Rainier to be photographed by Paris Match. After more than an hour, the Prince appeared just as Kelly was about to give up and leave. The rest is history. Ever since her death at the age of 52, Grace Kelly has led a post-mortem double life that continues to fascinate and tantalise.

Perhaps the funniest anecdote concerning her liaisons is the one recalled by David Niven on television to Michael Parkinson. Remembering an awkward conversation with Prince Rainier in which the latter asked him who had been his most exciting lover, Niven began to say "Grace Kelly."

He caught himself in time and changed his answer to "Gracie Fields." Fortunately Rainier had never heard of Fields and thus didn't realize the unlikelihood of such an encounter, as reported by Daily Express.

"They were living in a gilded cage," says her one-time fiancé Cassini. By the late 1970s, Grace Kelly was spending part of each year on her own in Paris. She began to enjoy the company of younger men like Robert Dornhelm, an Austrian film director. Even as her hell-raising daughters consumed more of her time, her marriage occupied less of it.

The constraints of palace life were not always easy for Grace.

Kelly's ancient habits and insatiable sex appetite resurfaced once again, but this time, only young handsome men became her favorite dish. Her husband's secret service found out about Kelly-Dornhelm sex encounters in Paris, and reported what they knew to Prince Rainier, after they have compiled enough evidence on Grace Kelly's involvement with the young film director, and her other affairs with two men who worked at the hotel where she stayed for a while.

The Princess

On March 25, 2007, The New York Post published the following article: "AFFAIR DOOMED PRINCESS' PAL. Grace Kelly had an extramarital affair with the handsome, ad-exec hubby of her best friend and bridesmaid Carolyn Reybold - a fling that sent the statuesque Ford model's life spiraling out of control and into madness, a new bio of the beloved Hollywood beauty claims.

Wendy Leigh, author of "True Grace: The Life and Times of an American Princess," told Page Six that "Suzy" columnist Aileen Mehle confided to her about a note Kelly sent to Reybold.

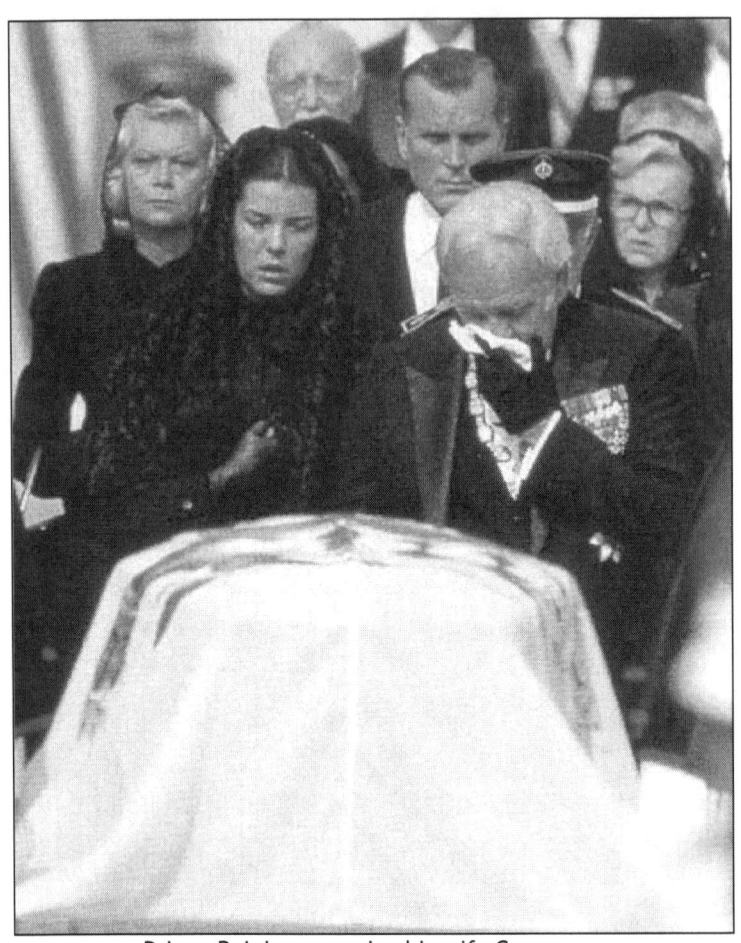
Prince Rainier mourning his wife Grace.

"In August 1960, I was at dinner and everyone was agog about the letter Princess Grace had written," Mehle told Leigh during her research for the book - a conversation Mehle confirmed to Page Six.

"It was a full confession to Carolyn, her friend and bridesmaid, telling her she loved her but she would never be happy, could never live with herself if she did not confess to Carolyn that she had had an affair with Carolyn's husband, Malcolm. She said she was sorry. She was seeking expiation."

As to her affair with Malcolm, wrong as it was, I believe that she succumbed to Malcolm, an accomplished seducer, at a time when she was vulnerable in the extreme. But receiving that letter from Grace was the beginning of the downfall of Carolyn." Leigh also writes of affairs Kelly is rumored to have had with Marlon Brando and Frank Sinatra. "She had a great deal of romantic opportunities and she could hardly be blamed for taking them," Leigh said. "She was the world's first liberated woman - and besides, Rainier was so unfaithful."

Grace Kelly with Jimmy Stewart.

This is what Jimmy Stewart had to say at her funeral: "You know, I just love Grace Kelly.
Not because she was a princess, not because she was an actress, not because she was my friend, but because she was just about the nicest lady I ever met.
Grace brought into my life as she brought into yours, a soft, warm light every time I saw her, and every time I saw her was a holiday of its own. No question, I'll miss her, we'll all miss her, God bless you, Princess Grace." - Jimmy Stewart at the funeral of Grace Kelly.

Grace Kelly's multiple lovers, to name a few:

- Alexander D'Arcy
- Aly Khan
- Anthony Curtis
- Anthony Quinn
- Bing Crosby
- David Niven
- Don Richardson
- Frank Sinatra
- Fred Zinnemann
- Gary Cooper
- Jean-Pierre Aumont
- Judy Garland
- Mark Miller
- Marlon Brando
- Josephine Baker
- Oleg Cassini
- Paul Newman
- Pierre Galante
- Ray Milland
- Robert Dornhelm
- Shah of Iran
- Victor Mature
- William Holden
- Jimmy Stewart

When Josephine Baker passed away, Princess Grace arranged for her to be buried in Monaco. Grace Kelly is shown here in a black dress, in the front row at Josephine Baker's state funeral.

The Stud Sex-Maniacs

Errol Flynn
John Barrymore
Charlie Chaplin
James Stewart
Gary Cooper
Spencer Tracy (For a while)
William Holden
Irving Thalberg
Howard Hughes

1- William Holden: He died on November 16, 1981 from injuries caused by a fall on 535 Ocean Avenue, Santa Monica, California, following a heavy drinking secret girlfriends: French actress, Capucine who committed suicide, Grace Kelly who had numerous affairs, and Audrey Hepburn. Holden was number 6 on the list of "Grace Kelly's lovers" compiled by the secret service of Prince Rainier III of Monaco (her future husband.) The list was long and included 43 certified lovers, major and minor stars.

Spencer Tracy: He remained married to Louise Treadwell until his death, despite his passionate relationship with actress Katharine Hepburn. Had numerous extra-marital affairs. Proposed anal sex to Vivien Leigh, and Irene Dunne.

Gary Cooper: He had numerous affairs with Hollywood's leading ladies. Among his mistresses were: Tallulah Bankhead, Grace Kelly, Patricia Neal, and Ingrid Bergman. His well-known girlfriends were: Carol Lombard, Marlene Dietrich (who said he was an idiot), and volatile Lupe Velez, known for seriously scratching the face of her husband Johnny Weissmuller. Velez Lupe said "Coop has the biggest dick in town."

John Barrymore: With a penchant for alcohol, voyeurism, kinky sex, the Gibson Girls, and chorus girls, Barrymore, the sick sex maniac character, was the one who deflowered both young actress Mary Astor when she was 17 year old, in his dressing room, and allegedly the 16 year old Floradora chorus girl Evelyn Nesbit who got her pregnant twice.

John Barrymore with wife Elaine Barrie.

On the surface, John Barrymore appeared as a savvy, perfect gentleman with savoir faire and "bonne mannieres." In true life, Barrymore was a pig, a pervert, and a sex maniac, with insatiable sexual-bestial appetite. In 1924, the beautiful 17 year old virgin, Mary Astor arrived to Hollywood. The first to spot her was none but John "The Wolf" Barrymore. Did I say Wolf? You bet. Astor was the lamb, and Barrymore the tricky wolf. Barrymore was mesmerized by Astor's candid beauty, innocence, and by what he called "her sexual naiveté!" Wow! Thus, he recommended her to Warners, and convinced them to cast her as his co-star in "Beau Brummel" (1924). The young Mary Astor was impressed, and very grateful. Twenty four hours after signing her contract with Warners, John Barrymore made his move; he invited her to his suite in Biltmore Hotel, where the young and "naïve" Mary Astor delivered herself to his sexual caprices. They become lovers, and in gratitude Astor became his "sex slave".

Chorus girl Evelyn Nesbit, allegedly deflowered by Barrymore when she was 16 year old. Others have said, it was Stanford White, who did it!

Adios Astor's virginity!! At the beginning, the young Astor believed that Barrymore was really in love with her, little did she know, that behind her back, John "The Wolf" Barrymore was already sleeping with the 19 year old Dolores Costello, his co-star in the 1925 film "The Sea Beast"; a very a propos title! Astor caught him in the act, and without any embarrassment, the wolf told the lamb to forget about him, because he is a son of a bitch.

John Barrymore with Mary Astor in "Beau Brummel," 1924. Barrymore also deflowered Astor when she was 17 or 18 year, in his dressing room.

A few months later, Barrymore abandoned Costello, and started looking for new victims. In 1932, he met young Katharine Hepburn, and as usual, using the same technique, convinced the studio to cast Hepburn as his co-star in "A Bill of Divorcement." This was Hepburn's film debut. The déjà vu experience repeated itself; here is Barrymore inviting Hepburn to lunch in his dressing room.
She accepted.
Once inside his dressing room, Barrymore locked the door, and began to take his clothes off. Totally naked, he approached Hepburn and tried to grab her breasts. She screamed: "Back off, my father does not want me to have any babies!" She put him in his place.

The Shakespearean wrote: "By the mid-1930s, however, years of hard living, reckless drinking, and a mercurial disregard for his personal well-being had taken their toll.
Barrymore began to experience numerous alcohol-related illnesses, and his memory became increasingly erratic; on several occasions, he found himself unable to remember his lines.

In 1935, he began a relationship with a starstruck 19-year-old college student, Elaine Barrie, later to become his fourth wife. Their bizarre liaison resulted in sensational tabloid headlines as this young "Ariel" pursued her "Caliban" (as the press dubbed them) across the country.
By that time, it was clear to the film community that Barrymore's skills and memory were in decline. Forced to read lines from blackboards placed just out of camera range, he was cast mainly in secondary roles in inferior films as a parody of his former self. During the 1939-40 season, he made an ill-starred return to Broadway in *My Dear Children*, a flimsy, exploitative comedy in which he burlesqued his image as an over-the-hill ham.
On May 19, 1942, Barrymore collapsed during a rehearsal of the Vallee radio program. He died on May 29, at 10:20 P. M. in his sleep.
Each of them had a bottle sticking out of his coat pocket." At that time, Barrymore was living in a whorehouse, dressed like a homeless, and always unshaven.
The once upon a time, multi-millionaire and "The Great Barrymore", died flat broke, penniless, in 1942. It was a sad moment in the history of cinema and performing arts.

The Ziegfeld Girls who created a huge scandal!

Prerequisites to qualify:

- A "Great Ass"
- A "Firm Breast"
- Legs a la Dietrich
- A full display of natural assets
- Service at the "Casting Couch".

The most noted ones were:
- Dorothy Flood.
- Naomi Johnson.
- Adrienne Ames.
- Anonyma (Debbie).

See their photos on the next page.

***   ***   ***

Dorothy Flood from the Follies of 1921.   Naomi Johnson.

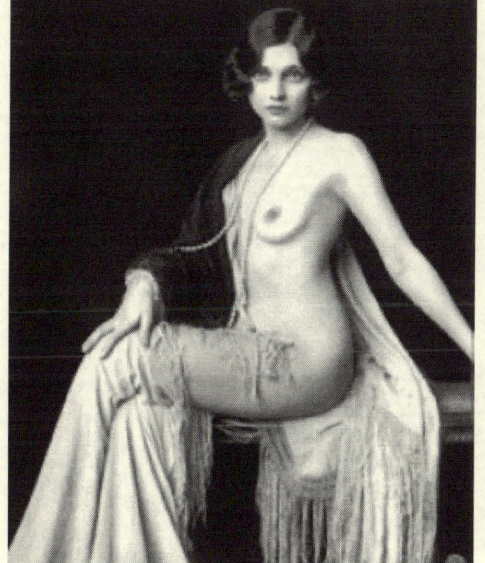 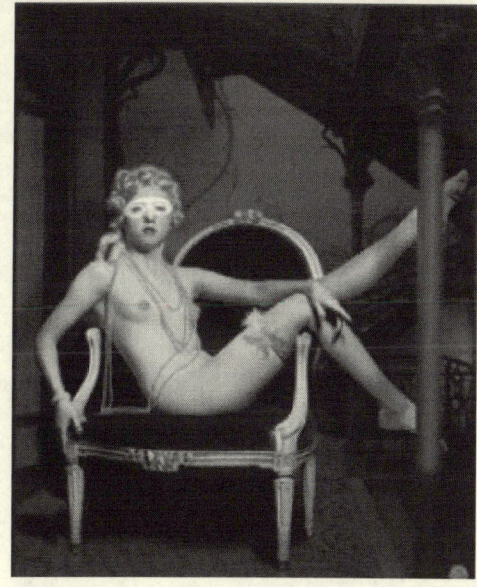

Adrienne Ames.   Anonyma

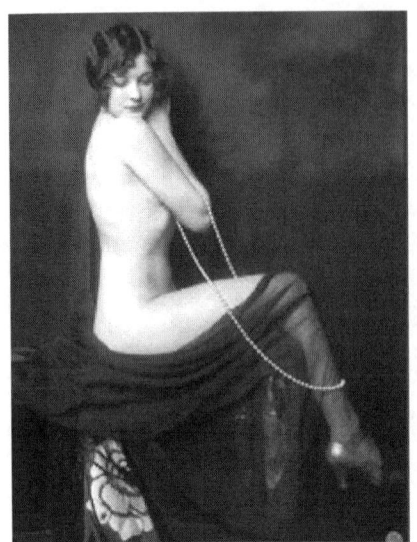
Marjorie King

Jean Ackerman

Muriel Finley

The Cutter Sisters

Vivian Porter

Marilyn Vega

Ann Lee Patterson

Anita Berber

And this what Hollywood's actresses (Beauties) do after hour!

A different kind of scandal
The May Irwin Kiss: The First Kiss on Film!

Thomas Alva Edison. No one can argue that he was not a tough and shrewd businessman.

Edison was the producer and cinematographer of May Irwin's film "The Kiss" that created the biggest cinematographic scandal of the era.

The film "The Kiss" also known as The May Irwin Kiss, The Rice-Irwin Kiss and The Widow Jones.
The film created a huge scandal, and stole the headlines and front pages of the newspapers of the era.
Articles, editorials and calls from "concerned citizens" demanded an immediate police action where the film was shown. "The Kiss" was directed by William Heise for Thomas Edison. In 1895, the biggest hit of the season was *The Widow Jones*, written by John J. McNally. May Irwin played the colorful role of a rich heiress, Beatrice Byke, fully dressed up as a thread-bare widow throwing fortune-hunting characters off her trail.
Co-star John C. Rice and May Irwin engaged in an extended kiss. At that time in history, cinema was just getting started, and Thomas Edison was experimenting with movies. Edison asked both, May Irwin and John C. Rice if they would repeat their stage kiss scene for the camera, and to his delight they agreed without any hesitation. And from that moment, that 18 second piece of film was referred to (as well as titled) *The Widow Jones, simply* because of the scene was taken from the original play. The 18 second kissing scene caused an enormous uproar.

May Irvin being kissed by John C. Rice.

May Irwin was born on 27, 1862 in Whitby, Ontario, and died on October 22, 1938 in New York City.

Consequently massive campaigns against "deterioration of moral values" launched by preachers took the country by storm.

The film was first shown in West End Park, Ottawa, Canada. It premiered in the United States on June 26, 1896, at a 400-seat Vitascope Hall.

Admission was 10 cents.

The scandal did not affect the career of Irwin, nor had any negative impact on her recordings. May Irwin became a major star, and one of the most popular singers of her time. Her song "After the Ball Is Over" was one of the biggest hits of the era.

One contemporary critic wrote: "The spectacle of the prolonged pasturing on each other's lips was beastly enough in life size on the stage but magnified to gargantuan proportions and repeated three times over it is absolutely disgusting."

Thomas Edison wrote in his catalogue: "They get ready to kiss, begin to kiss, and kiss and kiss and kiss in a way that brings down the house every time."

The Casting Couch

During Hollywood's heyday, the casting couch was a revered institution.

In his excellent book "Sex lives of Hollywood Godesses", author Nigel Cawthorne wrote, that the Hollywood screen goddesses, however, did not confine their attentions to just their fellow actors. They were much more democratic than that.

Starlets, stars, and divas slept with producers, stunt men, lighting men, millionaires, playwrights, politicians, and even members of the general public and, of course, directors. Many stories have been told about the casting couch. Indeed, during Hollywood's heyday, it was a revered institution.

Most would-be actresses did not go unwillingly to the movie moguls' sofas. Most leapt at the chance.
Even outside the enchanted realm of Tinseltown, few women can resist the lure of wealth and powers.
The vows of fidelity were most definitely cut from the script of the average Hollywood romantic relationship and marriage. Vivien Leigh, star of "Gone with the Wind", once told a friend: "I am an actress, a great actress. Great actresses have lovers, why not? I have a husband and I have lovers, like Sarah Bernhardt."

Commitments and marriages in Tinseltown were not like commitments and marriages in the rest of the world. The words "till death do us part" had been cut by the script editor. And this paved the way to gang-bang, multiple sexual parters, and the casting couch.
What could be done, could easilly be undone.

*** *** ***

Florenz Ziegfeld was well known for his taste of young flesh, and no girl worked for him unless she graduated from the casting couch in his office.

Many Hollywood's marriages were over in the blinking of an eye. And there was always another one right around the corner, in a horny star's dressing room, and possibly on or under the casting couch. "People in Hollywood think marriage is a game of musical chairs", as Grace Kelly's father said.

Olive Thomas' sexual skills and the casting couch.

Olive Thomas came from a mining town in Pennsylvania where, at the age of ten, she started posing nude with her grown-up brothers for pornographic photographs.
She was married at twelve to a twenty-six-year-old miner who liked to show Olive Off naked to his drunken friends. Sometimes he would get her to give a demonstration of her sexual skills before an invited audience of pals.
At fourteen, she stole the bus fare and ran away to New York, where she made her way to the Ziegfeld Follies. Florenz Ziegfeld was well known for his taste of young flesh, and no girl worked for him unless she graduated from the casting couch in his office;

Olive Thomas

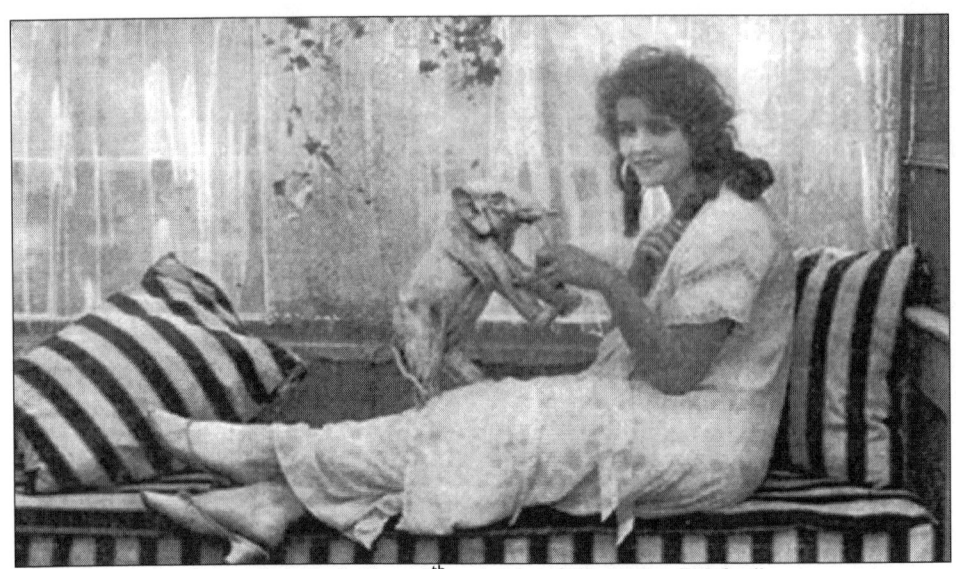
Olive Thomas in the 10th episode of "Beatrice Fairfax".

This genius beast slept with no less than 300 actresses, singers, and dancers.
Sometime, four women a day! Olive Thomas had no problem with this. Olive's early life left her with a craving for rough sex. This presented Ziegfeld with a problem as make-up could not always hide the welts and bruises on the body of his underaged star. The solution was to send her to Lewis J. Selznick.

Olive Thomas talking to Lewis J. Selznick: "So this is where I get laid?"

Most girls found Selznick's manner intimidating, but Olive Thomas walked straight up to his couch and said: "So this is where I get laid?" By that afternoon she was under contract and soon became a star as the virginal heroine of such movies as "Betty Takes a Hand", "Prudence on Broadway", and "The Follies Girl". As mentioned in Sex Lives of the Hollywood Goddesses.

Sarah Bernhardt as Lady Macbeth, circa 1884.

Is this what Sennett was talking about? Is this the kind of skin Sennett was talking about? I doubt it. I don't think he would have invited these four ladies to his casting couch!

Mack Sennett's Bathing Beauties casting couch?

Who was the first casting couch director? Sennett, Zanuck or Charlie Chaplin?

The 1917 Mack Sennett's Bathing Beauties were pin-up girls for the doughboys of the First World War.
Sennett's favorite bathing girls.
- Gloria Swanson,
- Marie Prevost,
- Phyllis Haver
- Mary Thurman

The Mac Sennett's roster of the Bathing Beauties included:
- Harriet Hammond,
- Charlie Murray,
- Mary Thurman,
- Juanita Hansen.

All these ladies were either lesbians or bisexuals.

Mack Sennett

Mack Sennett once said, he did not ask his girls to undress against their will, all women beautiful and ugly love to show off their skin.
Perhaps, but Mack Sennett was famous for his casting couch and his multiple orgies with his Bathing Beauties.

Were the tales about Mack Sennett's Bathing Beauties casting couch true? And were some of his girls, like Gloria Swanson, Carole Lombard, and Mabel Normand, part of his hand-picked harem? You bet!
In fact, Sennett invented the casting conch in 1912, as soon as he arrived to Los Angeles. According to Charlie Chaplin, it was Darryl F. Zanuck who first invented the casting couch. And according to Zanuck, it was Chaplin.

> David Smith wrote: "Zanuck was a workaholic, and despite his marriage, was an enthusiastic proponent of casting couch interviews, although never to the detriment of a production in the early years of his career; his notorious womanizing-by-appointment on the lot was seen as an outlet, something almost inconceivable today."

Phyllis Haver with Gloria Swanson

Chester Conklin with Mack Sennett's "Bathing Beauties."

Mac Sennett's Bathing Beauties: Charm, beauty, and a lot of sex!
Second row, from left to right: Harriet Hammond, Charlie Murray, Mary Thurman, Juanita Hansen. All these ladies were either lesbians or bisexuals.

Marie Prevost

Phyllis Haver

Carole Lombard

The Casting Couch!! Ouch!!

In "Shadowland" November 1921, novelist Theodore Dreiser published "Hollywood: Its Morals and Manners, Part One: The Struggle on the Threshold of Motion Pictures." In it he explained the "casting couch".

He wrote: "By far the greater number of girls and women who essay this work know very well beforehand via hearsay or exact information the character of the conditions to be met.
And if they do not know it beforehand, they could not be about the work a month before they would be aware of the general assumption of those connected with the work, the males in particular, of course, that all women connected with the work are potentially, if not actually, of easy virtue.

Therefore, if they resent this and still linger about the scene, ambition or not, the responsibility is at least in part theirs. And a very large number linger, not only quite willingly, even though they may possess ample means to go elsewhere if they choose, but they rather relish, I think, the very lively war that is here persistently on between the sexes.

hey are by no means innocents or lambs being led to the slaughter. And not a few relish the personal and emotional freedom which life in this realm provides."

Charlie Chaplin was probably one of the first stars to make systematic use of the casting couch for sexual ammunition.

According to leading film historian Kevin Brownwing, author of "The Golden Grope: A History of Hollywood Harassment", (Word for word): Famed silent comedian Charlie Chaplin was probably one of the first stars to make systematic use of the 'casting couch' for sexual gratification.
"Apparently he would only communicate with the actresses he was 'auditioning' via caption cards and mime, supposedly to test their ability to 'perform' in silent movies," says Brownwing.

"The cards would become ever more lewd and suggestive as he got them to undress, and he would fondle their breasts in an exaggerated silent movie acting manner, silently conveying his growing sexual arousal through grotesque facial mugging and crudely mimed gestures.
Eventually, he would get them to stand, naked, at one end of the audition room and throw custard pies at them. Finally, he would lick the girls clean with his tongue before making love to them on an actual casting couch, whilst a pianist played appropriate background music.

*** *** ***

Chaplin's casting couch's stars and starlets, and sex partners (To name a few):

1. Mildred Harris. He did her when she was 16 year old. Finally, he married her to save his neck, and due to a pregnancy. Harris was one of the sexual partners of Alla Nazimova.
2. Mary Pickford.
3. Peggy Hopkins Joyce.
4. Marion Davies, the mistress of William Randolph Hearst. Davies did not graduate from Chaplin's couch.
5. Edna Purviance.
6. Josephine Dunn.
7. Lila Lee.
8. Anna Q. Nilson.
9. Claire Windsor.
10. Pola Negri.
11. Gloria Swanson. (He did her out of curiosity. And she did him for the same reason; probably to put her seal of approval on his legendary sex-mania.)
12. May Collins.
13. Thelma Morgan Converse.
14. Clare Sheridan.
15. Paulette Goddard. He married her due to a pregnancy.
16. Lillita McMurray (Lita Grey). She was 16 when he took her virginity. He married her to avoid criminal prosecution, and due to a pregnancy.
17. Clara Bow.
18. Alla Nazimova.
19. Sari Maritza.
20. 21. Carole Landis.
21. Joan Berry.
22. Hetty Kelly, when she was 15 year old.
23. Oona Chaplin (He married her, when she was 17.)
24. Billie Dove.

*** *** ***

From left to right: Gloria Swanson, Charles Chaplin and Marion Davies at the premiere of "City Lights" in Los Angeles on 30 January 1931. He did them both!!

Hetty Kelly.
Chaplin did her when she was 15 year old.

Edna Purviance

Chaplin with wife Paulette Goddard.
One of the many wives of Chaplin.

Lita Grey, one of the many wives of Chaplin.

Below: Mildred Harris and Billie Dove in "The Heart of a Follies Girl" (1928)

Fingerprinting Charlie Chaplin, like a criminal. Was he innocent? Many believe so!

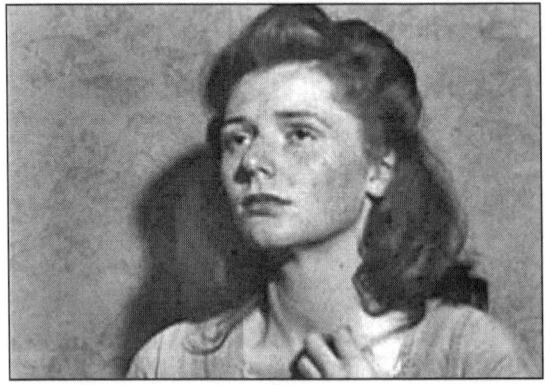

Femme fatale, Joan Barry, who got Chaplin in trouble. She accused him of raping her.

Joan Barry said that in October, 1942, she had gone to New York City at Chaplin's expense, had been followed by him, and had had relations with him in his hotel room.
From what it was written in the media: "This meant that Chaplin could be prosecuted under the Mann Act, a federal law which made it a serious crime (up to 25 years in prison and a fine of $25,000) to transport a female across a state line for immoral purposes.
Originally aimed at organized prostitution ("white slavery"), the Mann Act was also used as a sort of "interstate intercourse act," a way of prosecuting people the authorities wanted to "get" for some other, not necessarily criminal reason."

An attorney questioning Joan Barry.

Stephen Weissma reported: "At the time, 52 year old Charlie Chaplin signed Joan Barry to the renewable six month studio contract complete with acting lessons at the classy Max Rheinhardt School, and swanky Beverly Hills dentistry to cap her teeth—he considered her a gifted and promising actress."

Is the casting couch still up and running?
While the starlets insist they've never been offered or promised a role in exchange for a roll in the hay, one admits – off the record, please – "the casting couch isn't entirely a myth – it really does go on." But don't pity the poor aspiring actress who's actually putting out. "It's really a two-way street, you know," she says. "It has never ever been a bad thing in Hollywood to be sleeping with a director who's just won an Oscar or the hot new movie star whose face is on the cover of *Time* magazine."

Do starlets sleep with a lot of Hollywood studs?
The short answer: Yes. Long days on the set, sometimes doing love scenes, and breed intimacy keep you from meeting guys elsewhere, say the starlets. Plus, industry parties are the place to be and operate as Hollywood's unofficial singles-bar scene. Let's name names: Wuhrer confesses to getting *cozy* briefly with her *Crossing Guard* director Sean Penn and dating Jason Patric, now Christy Turlington's main man.
Marcil is no stranger to star-crossing either. She's currently dating her former *General Hospital* costar Tyler Christopher, was married for a few minutes to actor Corey Feldman back in the early '90s, and was reported to be romantically linked to her famous friend, the artist formerly known as Prince.

Do outrageously sexy things go on all the time at Hollywood parties?
It definitely seems as if it's hard to keep one's clothes on at a private fete in Tinseltown. Wuhrer confesses to climbing onstage at a *Paper* magazine party, singing the blues, and then stripping down to her underwear before jumping in a pool. She also boasts, "Last week I played Truth or Dare at the Château Marmont hotel with Jim Sheridan and Timothy Hutton and stuck my naked butt out the window."
Adds another starlet: "I've been to parties with topless girls serving hors d'oeuvres, tons of them where there has been skinny-dipping, and usually anytime you walk into the bedroom of a Hollywood player during a party, there's a naked girl waiting for him under the covers." (Source: As reported by Michael Lewittes in Cosmopolitan magazine.)

***   ***   ***

Hollywood Sex Pests

Don Johnson

Steven Seagal

Arnold Schwarzenneger

"Arnold Schwarzenneger, Don Johnson, Steven Seagal - just a handful of the Hollywood celebrities who have stood accused of sexual harassment in recent years. However, such allegations are nothing new in Tinseltown.

The use of the casting couch by powerful male industry figures to extract sexual services from young female performers struggling to gain a foot hold in the business has become something of a Hollywood tradition - stretching back to the silent era."

*** *** ***

The Casting Couch Big Names

The most notorious casting couch directors

- Ben Schulberg
- Charlie Chaplin
- Flo Ziegfeld
- George Preston Marshall
- George White
- Harry Cohn
- Howard Hughes
- Irving Thalberg
- John Barrymore
- Lewis J. Selznick
- Mac Sennett
- Raymond Griffith

Ben Schulberg

Charlie Chaplin

Flo Ziegfeld

George Preston Marshall

George White

Harry Cohn

Howard Hughes

Irving Thalberg

John Barrymore (He was an actor)

Lewis J. Selznick

Mac Sennett

Raymond Griffith

From left to right: Irving Thalberg, his wife Norma Shearer and Louis B Mayer.

Thalberg was notorious for his extramarital affairs, casting couch, and orgies. Mayer who has once said, "An actress ass belongs to her husband, not to the public", also has said, "Nothing matters, nothing matters."

Photo: Anita Page.

Louis B. Mayer Mayer owned a bordello that catered to Hollywood law enforcement units, and the stars who were under his contract.

In a 2004 interview with author Scott Feinberg, Anita Page said, that her refusal to meet demands for sexual favors by MGM head of production, Irving Thalberg, who was married to Norma Shearer, supported by Studio chief Louis B. Mayer, is what truly ended her career

---

Howard Hughes Lovers and Sex Partners

According to insiders, Hughes has slept with at least 200 movie stars. To name a few:

Corinne Griffith	Barbara Hutton
Madge Bellamy	Arleene Whelan
Constance Bennett	Bete Davis
Ella Rice	Ingrid Bergman
Jean Harlow	Jane Greer
Ida Lupino	Lana Turner
Joan Crawford	Gail Russell
Evelyn Brent	Yvonne De Carlo
Frances Drake	Virginia Mayo
Marguerite Chapman	Ann Miller
Olivia de Haviland	Ava Gardner
Barbara Stanwyck	Linda Darnell
Norma Shearer	Terry Moore
Helen Gilbert	Mamie van Doren
Andrea Leeds	Marlene Dietrich
Jean Fontaine	Jean Peters
Gloria Vanderbilt	Barbara Lawrence
Faith Domergue	Faye Emerson
Cyd Charisse	Jean Wallace
Brenda Frazier	Barbara Payton
Mona Freeman	Corinne Griffith
Paulette Goddard	Madge Bellamy
Sheila Ryan	Constance Bennett
Jane Russell	Ella Rice
Marian Marsh	Jean Harlow
Lillian Bond	Ida Lupino
Billie Dove	Joan Crawford
Dorothy Jordan	Evelyn Brent
Ginger Rogers	Frances Drake
Katharine Hepburn	Marguerite Chapman
June Lang	Olivia de Haviland
Nancy Carroll	Barbara Stanwyck
Barbara Pepper	Norma Shearer
Merle Oberlon	Helen Gilbert
Blanche Sweet	Shelley Winters
Carole Lombard	Andrea Leeds

Jean Fontaine	Ingrid Bergman
Gloria Vanderbilt	Jane Greer
Mitzi Gaynor	Lana Turner
Faith Domergue	Renee Adoree
Cyd Charisse	Gail Russell
Brenda Frazier	Yvonne De Carlo
Mona Freeman	Virginia Mayo
Mary Astor	Ann Miller
Paulette Goddard	Ava Gardner
Sheila Ryan	Thelma Todd
Jane Russell	Linda Darnell
Marian Marsh	Terry Moore
Lillian Bond	Mamie van Doren
Billie Dove	Marlene Dietrich
Dorothy Jordan	Jean Peters
Ginger Rogers	Ann Dvorak
Rita Hayworth	Barbara Lawrence
Katharine Hepburn	Faye Emerson
June Lang	Jean Wallace
Nancy Carroll	Barbara Payton
Barbara Pepper	Zsa Zsa Gabor
Merle Oberlon	Eleanor Boardman
Blanche Sweet	Ella Rice
Peggy Knudson	Constance Bennett
Carole Lombard	Veronica Lake
Barbara Hutton	Virginia Bruce
Arleene Whelan	Zizi Jeanmaire
Phyllis Brooks	Tallulah Bankhead
Bete Davis	Susan Peters
Pola Negri	

Joan Harlow Ida Lupino Joan Crawford Evelyn Brent
Corinne Griffith Madge Bellamy Constance Bennett Ella Rice

Howard Hughes with Ginger Rogers. (Data: Who Dated Who; Hollywood Classic.)

Books by Maximillien de Lafayette in this Area

The New Mega: Hollywood Earth Shattering Scandals.
4 Volumes (9th Edition)

Cover of Book 1

Cover of Book 2

Cover of Book 3

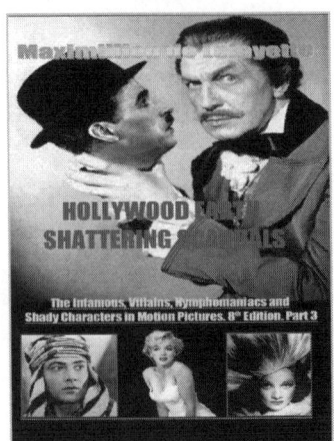

Cover of Book 4

NOTES

NOTES

Published by
Times Square Press
New York Berlin

Printed in the United States of America